T0194131

Greed, Power
AND Politics

The Dismal History of Economics and the
Forgotten Path to Prosperity

DANIEL CAMERON

WESTBOW
PRESS®
A DIVISION OF THOMAS NELSON
& ZONDERVAN

Copyright © 2018 Daniel Cameron.
For further information contact the author at dancameron04@gmail.com

This book is a work of non-fiction. Unless otherwise noted, the author
and the publisher make no explicit guarantees as to the accuracy of
the information contained in this book and in some cases, names
of people and places have been altered to protect their privacy.

All rights reserved. No part of this book may be used or reproduced by
any means, graphic, electronic, or mechanical, including photocopying,
recording, taping or by any information storage retrieval system
without the written permission of the author except in the case of
brief quotations embodied in critical articles and reviews.

WestBow Press books may be ordered through booksellers or by contacting:

WestBow Press
A Division of Thomas Nelson & Zondervan
1663 Liberty Drive
Bloomington, IN 47403
www.westbowpress.com
1 (866) 928-1240

Because of the dynamic nature of the Internet, any web addresses or
links contained in this book may have changed since publication and
may no longer be valid. The views expressed in this work are solely those
of the author and do not necessarily reflect the views of the publisher,
and the publisher hereby disclaims any responsibility for them.

Any people depicted in stock imagery provided by Getty Images are
models, and such images are being used for illustrative purposes only.
Certain stock imagery © Getty Images.

ISBN: 978-1-9736-2858-3 (sc)
ISBN: 978-1-9736-2857-6 (e)

Print information available on the last page.

WestBow Press rev. date: 5/16/2018

To my beloved wife and daughters, Jessica, Lauren and Lindsay

Contents

Acknowledgements

This book would not have been possible without the support and encouragement from my family, especially my wife Jessica. As a history teacher her insights have been invaluable. I would also like to give a special thanks to my brother Jim for countless hours of editing and polishing a rather rough first draft, and for his professional advice and assistance. Finally, thanks to my brother Tom for our many hours of history related conversations. Of course, all the opinions reflected in this book are my own.

INTRODUCTION

Private Property, Communism and Adam Smith

Private property evolved when people domesticated animals and tilled the soil. This allowed them to move from tents or thatched huts into permanent homes; and led from day to day subsistence to an economy where a surplus of perishable goods could be exchanged for labor, commodities or finished goods. Initially, this was accomplished through bartering and later through the exchange of a commodity that held a commonly accepted value, now referred to as money.

The changes in society that led to private property and an exchange economy allowed cities to grow because farmers could simply go to a central market and sell their surplus produce or meat to artisans, tradesmen or laborers, who earned money from selling their products or labor. It was no longer necessary for everyone to live directly off the land. Cities simply grew outward from the central markets, which became flooded with people.

Unfortunately, cities, permanent homes, and specialized labor had some serious drawbacks: famines from droughts caused mass starvation because people could not easily move to new hunting grounds or more fertile lands; and even if they did, most of them lacked the necessary skills to find and process food. In addition to the civil aspects of urban living, there were also such public necessities as clean water, sewage and waste disposal, though critically important, were grossly inadequate. Rodents carrying millions of plague-infested fleas spread the dreaded Bubonic Plague. Striking the

Roman Empire in the Sixth Century, the *Black Death* killed at least 50 million people; then, striking again in the Fourteenth Century, a third of Europe's population was decimated.

Also, grossly inadequate was the fair administration of justice. Through fear and brutality, rulers could establish arbitrary laws and accumulate great wealth through confiscation and taxation. As populations grew, rulers could use this wealth to pay and equip large numbers of men to armed service, leading to conquest, slavery, empire building, and often mass destruction.

None of this civilizing would have occurred, however, if not for the concept of *surplus*. Before, if a family or tribe produced more food than it could eat, then the food simply spoiled and went to waste. Because of the central market, surplus produce could be sold to willing buyers. Therefore, rather than having a surplus of spoiled food, one could exchange fresh perishable foods for money, which could be used to purchase better tools or weapons, hire workers, and acquire more land. This process necessitated what we now call *Specialization of Labor*. One could become an expert in some specialized field of endeavor and sell his or her labor or products made by hand. These concepts lead us to an important principle: natural resources have no economic value without human labor and human ingenuity. This is just as true whether the process is as simple as picking fruit or as complicated as manufacturing a computer.

The aforementioned assumes that there was a demand in the market for all this extra meat, produce, labor or products and that consumers were willing to pay a price high enough to cover costs and provide a nice profit, which could be saved, re-invested or used to provide a more comfortable standard of living. As the populations expanded, so did the size and scope of potential markets, which in turn increased the number and size of producers. This process continued until equilibrium between supply and demand was achieved, which of course became a moving target as populations fluctuated, tastes changed and new markets opened up.

Was any of this necessary? What if everyone already had shelter and clothing, and food was in abundance? In pre-European Tahiti, no one cared. Plenty of food was available for anyone who wished to pick it off the tree or catch it from the ocean; clothing was optional and shelter consisted of a thatched hut. Life was good! There was no Per capita Income or Gross Domestic Product, so why can't the whole world be like that?

Part of the answer is scarcity. In most parts of the world winters are uninhabitable without warm clothes and shelter for both humans and domesticated animals. In addition, growing seasons are relatively short, which requires either large quantities of stored or imported foods. The other part of the answer was discussed earlier: civilization itself -- large, diverse populations of strangers living in permanent dwellings and surrounded by cities. There was no longer a transient, close knit tribe that fed, clothed and protected its members.

In comparing the various modern economic systems, we can assume that the concepts of money, production, distribution and consumption are really all related to one question: How do societies distribute goods and services to large populations when these resources are scarce and require high levels of coordinated effort, tools, and an investment in either public or private capital?

Pre-European Tahiti

Try to imagine the European discovery of Tahiti. Lieutenant Samuel Wallis peering through his telescope on a bright, clear day in June of 1767. What he saw must have seemed like a dream. First, mountains jutted dramatically from an endless expanse of ocean, then hills and valleys came into view, covered with lush green foliage. As the ship approached closer to the island, palm fronds could be seen swaying in a gentle breeze as waves lapped lazily against the crystalline shore.

After a brief confrontation with the natives, peaceful relations were established between these two very different cultures. One of the first recorded observations was that even though Tahitians had no concept of private property, the people were happy, healthy and generous. There were no extremes in temperature; fresh food and water were in abundance, and life was safe and secure. Their social order and laws, or *Taboos*, were built around a homogeneous culture that had existed for some ten thousand years. The worst punishment was to be exiled -- expelled from the tribe -- and sent off to live a life of solitude in the cold mountains of the island's interior [3].

So, while there is no evidence of an innate human yearning for private property, there is a desire to improve one's condition and position in society and to have a degree of control; including the exercise of free will over our environment, our bodies, our parenting, our relationships, and our lives in order to make life easier and more comfortable.

Private Property

Private property can be viewed as an extension of, and a return on, a person's investment in labor. In the free-enterprise system, a worker is willing to commit to your company a certain number of hours per day of her time, energy and talent (labor) to further your company's goals. In exchange, you will pay her an agreed upon amount of money that can be used to further her goals. The more perceived value a person has to her employer, the higher her wages. Of course, however, this is relative to the supply of comparable labor in a given market. If the money that results from this wage is invested wisely, wealth (private property) will increase. This can be compared to a product, in that the more perceived value a product has to a consumer, the higher the price (again relative to supply); and the higher the price relative to the costs of production, the higher the profits. If the profits are invested wisely, the company becomes wealthier (more private property). And if you replace the word society with the words company and employee, then you can begin to see that all of the combined work and productive processes only benefit the worker and employer because society has placed a higher value on the services and products than their costs to society.

The fact that the builder, the butcher or the plumber is working for personal financial gain or that the corporate executive is working to further his company's profitability does not diminish the value that each has provided their employers, employees or customers. Otherwise they would be either unemployed or out of business. In essence, this is Adam Smith's *Invisible Hand Theory*. (We will further explore Adam Smith later in the chapter.)

Now if you extrapolate these ideas as an economic system, then new and improved products and services are continuously being introduced. Those that fall to the wayside are those that are valued less by consumers (society). This process is sometimes called *Creative Destruction*. While the system may seem cruel, at least to those whose jobs have been displaced or who have failed in their business ventures, it actually raises the quality of life and standard of living for everyone. The wealth that results from this system is the wealth that supports charities and pays taxes that fund government programs.

Therefore, in a free society many people believe that private property should be included as a basic human right; meaning that governments should never be allowed to take or destroy an individual's property without following due process of law. It also means that governments provide protection to its citizens from theft or vandalism. These concepts necessitate a fair and equitable justice system.

Communism

This brings up an important distinction between free enterprise and communism. In a commune, all basic necessities of life are provided by the commune and a person's labor is, in effect, a return on the investment made by the commune. Every able-bodied member contributes to the success of the commune. If it's assets grow, the benefits of those assets are shared equally among the members. Therefore, there is no private property, only communally-shared property.

Can Communism Be A Good Thing?

A certain degree of communism has been shown to work as an acceptable form of government in homogenous collectives that evolve from a common culture or religion; where members share similar values, come together voluntarily to live as a communal group, and are willing to work together toward common goals. However, in larger, more diverse societies there exists the necessity of forcing upon individuals the imposition of one giant, centralized collective that strips away innovation, enterprise, free associations, and differing values and beliefs.

There are certainly examples of private property in some primitive societies, just as there are examples of communism. All societal structures were and are based on the culture, history and values of the collective in question, not whether there was a natural yearning for private property on the one hand or communal living arrangements on the other.

Natural Law

For either communism or the free enterprise system to work there must be an assumption that human nature is basically moral. In other words, if everyone is out to cheat, steal or cause harm, then political systems falls apart. Natural Law proponents contend that all systems of law should comport with the basic laws of human nature. This theory makes the assumption that humans are essentially lawful, rational beings, who have basic rights that cannot be taken away by government. For example, in the Declaration of Independence, Thomas Jefferson *(1743-1826)* asserts: *We hold these truths to be self-evident, that all men are created equal, that they are endowed by their Creator with certain unalienable Rights, that among these are Life, Liberty and the pursuit of Happiness.* Jefferson borrowed these ideas from the philosopher, John Locke *(1632-1704)*, who believed that people were born equal and independent, and that everyone had and has a natural right to defend his life, health, liberty, and possessions.

Adam Smith

I think it's a good time to explore some ideas that have been around for a few hundred years but are largely ignored by world leaders today. Adam Smith *(1723-1790)* was an ethicist, as well as a political and economic philosopher, most famous for his book: *An Inquiry into The Nature and Causes of the Wealth of Nations (1776).* In his book, Smith explains that:

> *Little else is requisite to carry a state to the highest degree of opulence from the lowest barbarism, but peace, easy taxes, and a tolerable administration of justice; all the rest being brought about by the natural course of things. All governments which thwart this natural course, which force things into another channel, or which endeavor to arrest the progress of society at a particular point, are unnatural, and to support themselves are obliged to be oppressive and tyrannical.*

In other words, political stability based on the principles of natural law will bring about economic stability, leading to a state of affluence. A necessary element of this growth comes from trade, including international trade, not only for its extrinsic value, but also intrinsic values such as learning better ways of doing things; also, economic relations lead naturally to peaceful relations, mutual understanding and enrichment through cultural exchange. Smith also emphasized that both efficiencies and productivity will be enhanced by the **Division of Labor** and a continuous drive to improve methods and processes.

Smith defined wealth simply as well-being, expressed in arts, crafts and civility; in other words, the opposite of war, oppression, social stratification, or anything that keeps people down. He recognized that predation, violence, or the subjugation of other people inhibits economic growth. Why, Smith would ask, be industrious if someone can simply come along and destroy your property or take it from you? He believed that the tendency toward predation is part of human nature and must be guarded against. Smith further believed that governments are an essential part of

society and function best when they provide for defense, large
infrastructure projects, and the administration of justice, including
the enforcement of private property rights; then governments should
leave their people alone.

CHAPTER ONE

Mercantilism: Of Kings and Gold

We will have two simple rules when it comes to this country:
Buy American and Hire American... We will defeat the
enemy on jobs and we have to look at it almost as a war.
President Elect Donald Trump (1946-) at a North Carolina rally. December 6, 2016

Economic warfare is not a new concept. Mercantilism has its roots in Renaissance Europe and while it ultimately proved disastrous, vestiges have continued, even into the 21st century.

Let's begin with Jean-Baptiste Colbert *(1619-1683)*, Minister of Finances for King Louis XIV *(1638-1715)*. It was his guidance that led France from the brink of bankruptcy to that of an economic powerhouse -- at least temporarily. He rooted out and eliminated corruption and inefficiency in the tax collection process, and by closing loopholes was effective in taxing the rich. He also encouraged manufacturing, demanded high quality from producers, and implemented important economic reforms [1]. But, from a historical perspective, his real significance was being the most dominant practitioner of economic warfare or mercantilism.

The philosophical underpinnings for this system consist of five basic assumptions: First, there is only a fixed and limited amount of wealth in the world. If this is true then every international transaction is a *Zero-sum Gain* (or "Game"). (a Zero-sum Gain is when one person's gain is equivalent to another person's loss so the net change in wealth is zero.) For example, if France wanted to become wealthier, then it needed to find a country with wealth and take it from them. Now this could be accomplished by military conquest, or it could be accomplished by international trade, which brings us back to our topic at hand: economic warfare. Second, true wealth consists primarily of gold, silver or land. Third, self-interest is anti-social. Therefore, the interests of the crown (or state) should always be placed ahead of our own selfish personal interests. Fourth, business should be conducted by government-granted monopolies, also called *Grants of Exclusive Privilege* or in French, *De jure Monopoly.* Under these arrangements, highly lucrative and well connected oligarchical companies operate completely unfettered by competition, as mandated by law [2].

Jean-Baptiste Colbert was an adherent to a new breed of economic thinkers who were influenced by Isaac Newton and the Age of Enlightenment. If, they believed, the entire universe could be explained through scientific principles, then why not use scientific methods to control society? Louis the XIV was the epitome of an absolute monarch and as such was obsessed with amassing great amounts of wealth and power. So, control was exactly what he wanted and his method was through the use of government regulations. If a nation could manage and control a nation's resources and people during times of war, then why not use similar methods to also manage and control the nation during times of peace, and of course, control it all from France's center of power: his majesty, King Louis XIV? Then, blend a combination of government regulations, military and economic warfare to simultaneously weaken your international rivals and take their money to enrich yourself. Voila, mercantilism [3]!

International Trade

To explain this requires a brief lesson in 17th century international trade. If, for example, you were an English wine merchant who periodically traveled across the English Channel to re-stock your shelves, you had a problem with your English money, *Pounds Sterling,* which the French exporter could not spend in France because the French had their own currency, *Francs*. To solve this problem, the French and English, along with other countries, allowed their banks to accept the other nation's currency and exchange it for an equivalent amount of gold or silver. So, the English merchant got his wine and the French exporter got his French Francs and everyone was happy. However, to take the example further, we need to look at the French bank in possession of English Pound Sterling Notes. The bank, in conjunction with all of the French banks holding English currency, would periodically total up all of their Pound Sterling Notes, take them to England, and redeem them for actual sterling silver or an equivalent amount of gold. A Pound Sterling Note would be exchanged for a pound of actual sterling silver. This process would likewise be reversed in France. If, in a given year and by coincidence you had an exact balance of trade, then each country would have transferred to the other exactly the same value of gold and/or silver.

The French believed that if they could export far more goods than they imported, then they would consequently increase their gold reserves at the expense of their rivals, which meant that France would have more money to pay her military and her impoverished rivals would have less, making them easy targets for conquest and plunder. It would also provide France with the money to finance the exploration and conquest of India, Africa, the Pacific islands and the Americas; then to colonize them in the name of France. This meant fighting not only indigenous populations, but also rival colonizers, like England, the Netherlands and Spain. Secondly, King Louis didn't want his people buying the produce and products of other countries. Instead, he wanted to protect the French farmers and craftsmen by forcing French consumers to buy only French stuff. Why should Frenchmen enrich the farmers and manufacturers of some other country, sending their hard-earned money into the hands of the enemy? At the same time, he wanted to encourage exports to his rival trading partners [4]. To accomplish these goals, King Louis reduced taxes on major exports and in some cases provided government subsidies; all designed to make his country's products and produce artificially cheap on the international markets. Next, he erected trade barriers, such as tariffs, to restrict imports of products into his country. And if these measures weren't harsh enough, he would ban the imports of certain products altogether. These policies were directed primarily against English and Dutch products, with the ultimate goal of making these countries economically dependent on France.

An important element of mercantilism was to exert absolute control over your colonies. If, France and England were at war in Europe; then your colonies would be forced to fight in America, Africa, and India as well. Also, force them to purchase products manufactured only in the mother country, then ship colonial produce only in boats manufactured in the mother country, and only to ports within the mother country (and of course force them to pay taxes to the mother country). In other words, don't treat your colonies as independent entities; but instead make them work for you [5].

Keep in mind that the colonies were subject to the absolute will of the Crown (and in the case of England, Parliament). The purpose of colonial imperialism was to extract slave labor, and raw materials like gold, silver, lumber, and useful minerals, as well as agricultural products like sugar, tobacco and cotton from militarily weak, underdeveloped lands. The next step was to ship the mother country's dregs of society to the colonies and let them fend for themselves or work as indentured servants, without the crown having to bear the social costs of welfare, crime or imprisonment [6].

It took England some time to figure out these new rules of international economics. In the mid-1600's they were consumed with civil war, which resulted in the beheading of their king, Charles I *(1600-1649)*. By this time, France had bounced back from its own devastating religious war in the 1590's. By the late 1690's, England had stabilized and was fully engaged in both military and mercantilist warfare.

Meanwhile in Spain, the King and Queen were spending money faster than it was coming in from the New World and were becoming quite annoyed by, and a little jealous of, the Conquistadors who had not only become fabulously wealthy but had the audacity to act as if they too were royalty. The Conquistadors had gone into partnership with the Crown and as such were able to keep for themselves a pretty big share of all the New World plunder. So, taking a page out of the mercantilist playbook, Spain simply annexed their portion of the Americas, nationalized all the assets and installed the Crown's own colonial administrators.

The economic warfare between the countries of Europe ignited trade wars, military confrontations, and the exploration of uncharted territories with the goal of exploiting their natural resources. This led to the imperialistic colonizing of Africa, India, North and South America, Australia and islands around the globe. Indigenous populations were killed, enslaved, or in other ways subjugated to the will of the conquering Europeans.

In case you're wondering how all this turned out, I can tell you in one word: Badly! Only 78 years after the death of King Louis XIV, his great, great grandson, King Louis XVI, along with his family and political supporters were executed. The king was only 38. The French Revolution ended the House of Bourbon, brought forth civil war and the Jacobin's *Reign of Terror*, which culminated in the military dictatorship of Napoleon Bonaparte *(1769-1821)*. England gave up its thirteen colonies of North America after losing the Revolutionary War, and by the mid 1800's had largely abandoned mercantilism as an economic system. It continued, however, to gobble up cheap natural resources from its remaining colonies.

Even though Spain took from the Aztecs and Incas about $500 billion in today's currency, it still went bankrupt in 1575, having squandered its New World wealth on fruitless wars, and by the early 1800's was ruled by Napoleon. Spain subsequently lost control of its South and Central American colonies through a series of wars for independence; instigated by descendants of the original Conquistadors who wanted to regain complete political and economic control of their former territories. Spain's final defeat came at the hands of the United States, after losing the Spanish-American War, which ended in 1898 with the signing of the *Treaty of Paris.* Even though Spain suffered a resounding defeat, the U.S. agreed to pay them $20,000,000 for the Philippines. They were forced, however, to give up Cuba, Puerto Rico and Guam. With the signing of this agreement the United States became a colonial power. Filipino nationalists, however, sought independence from their new colonial rulers, so fighting broke out two days before the U.S. Senate ratified the Treaty. The Philippine-American War lasted three years and caused the deaths of about 4,200 U.S. soldiers and 20,000 Filipino combatants. Worse yet were civilian casualties: some 200,000-people died from violence, famine and disease. The United States allowed the Philippines to become a commonwealth in 1935 and in 1945 recognized it as an independent state. Even afterwards the United States maintained its military bases on the island, and throughout the 20th century meddled in its internal politics. For example, the U.S. propped up the Ferdinand Marcos *(1917-1989)* regime throughout his 20-year reign as President of the Philippines, providing over $1 billion in military aid and hundreds of millions in economic aid, during which time Marcos siphoned off billions from the Philippine Treasury into his personal off-shore accounts. Even though he was ousted from office in 1986, the U.S. allowed him safe haven in Hawaii. Our government later charged him with racketeering, but to no avail, he died in 1989.

Vestiges of Mercantilism in the United States

The entire westward expansion of the United States was a process of colonization and military conquest, including Hawaii.

Today our government places import restrictions and tariffs on many imported products. In addition, subsidies and grants are commonly given to American manufacturers and growers of certain crops. And if our government doesn't like the actions of a rival nation, economic sanctions are a convenient substitute for military confrontation.

The world we live in today is largely the result of mercantilism and European Colonial expansion. The influx of cheap raw materials fueled the Industrial Revolution, which led to technological advancements and the modern economy.

While the standards of living for industrialized nations have benefited, the poorest nations of the world continue in poverty. As the economist, David Landis has written:

> ...the difference in income per head between the richest industrial nation, say Switzerland, and the poorest nonindustrial country, Mozambique, is about 400 to 1. Two hundred and fifty years ago, this gap between richest and poorest was perhaps 5 to 1 [7].

It's safe to say that without the exploration and eventual European habitation of previously unknown lands, the world would look much different than it does today -- both for good and bad.

Adam Smith vs. the Mercantilists

So, let's analyze the main ideas behind mercantilism and compare them to the views of Adam Smith.

1. The world's wealth is fixed.
    Smith believed that wealth increases every time there is a mutually advantageous transaction, which is enhanced by the division of labor and continuously improving production techniques [7].

2. Economic Nationalism
    Smith believed in economic internationalism. If every mutually advantageous transaction (whether domestic or international) increases wealth, then it stands to reason that in aggregate, the sum of all mutually beneficial transactions must also increase a nation's wealth [8].

3. Gold and silver constitute a nation's wealth.

Smith believed that gold and silver have value, but only to the extent that they are useful or desirable as commodities, and as money, in which case they hold a commonly accepted value that can be used as collateral in international transactions. Smith believed that true wealth is constituted by goods and services and that money is nothing more than a means to an end, not true wealth. In other words, money is like a claim-ticket to what we want -- goods and services. If you couldn't exchange money for goods and services, then it would be worthless. The paper *Fiat Money* that is issued by nations today has no intrinsic value. It, in essence, is nothing more than an IOU. Its value is only relative to the financial strength of the issuing government; in other words, the country's ability to manage its finances, primarily its debt [9].

It should be noted that the gold in the King's treasury did not belong to the Crown. It was held in the vaults to back the currency of France and actually belonged to all the holders of French money. The portion of gold that represented tax revenue is all that belonged to King Louis IV. It was this tax revenue that paid for government services and the French military. Smith was advocating that if you increase mutually beneficial trade, then economic activity is increased. By increasing economic activity, you also increase the taxes collected by the Crown. Therefore, economic activity is the key to increasing a nation's wealth, and to a financially successful government.

4. Government created monopolies.

Until Adam Smith, governments thought that monopolized market segments were the most efficient and desirable way to manage an economy. Smith acknowledged that although these "Grants of Exclusive Privilege" were beneficial to the politically connected business owners, they were a terrible idea. By reducing or eliminating competition, they increased costs to consumers, made the industries less competitive in international markets, and hurt the total potential employment of the industries affected. This, in turn, reduced the potential tax revenues going to the Crown [10].

5. Self-interest is anti-social. The interests of the Crown should be placed ahead of our own selfish personal interests.

Smith believed that it is human nature to want to better ourselves, to get ahead in life, and to leave our children and grandchildren in a better, more prosperous state. All of these aspirations are related to the profit motive and self-interest. When we do this in a peaceful, mutually beneficial way through trade, then it is a good thing [11].

CHAPTER TWO

Marxist Socialism: The Workers Revenge

*The theory of Communism may be summed up in
one sentence: Abolish all private property.*
Karl Marx

Marx

The Philosophical side of Karl Marx *(1818-1883)* believed that as humans, our sense of being, and purpose in life comes from relations with other people, not from our own activities. We are like herd animals; it is the herd that is important, not the individual animal. He was therefore a corporatist in the sense that we are all part of a larger body. Separation from others is a tragedy and goes against our human nature.

Practically, speaking, however, Marx was somewhere between an economic philosopher, a political agitator, and an apocalyptic prophet. He professed to see the future of mankind, and in that future workers were to face increasing torment, toil, poverty and oppression at the hands of their bourgeois masters, until one day the workers of the world would unite and overthrow their oppressors. So, Marx tells his followers: look I know things are bad, and they will get worse -- unless you follow my plan which is to revolt now!

Marx believed capitalism to be a doomed economic system, because in order to manufacture a product you need land, labor, and technology (tools). As technology improves, the capitalist will invest more in technology and less in labor, and as laborers become poorer they will revolt. He views Adam Smith's law of supply and demand this way: If the demand for a product goes up without a corresponding rise in supply, then the price increases. (Price = the market value of the per unit output.) Supply is influenced by factors of production, like tools and methodology. Therefore, due to the synergy of the production process the output is greater than the costs related to the sum of inputs. In other words, price less the cost of inputs = profit. Marx argues that labor shouldn't be included as simply part of the input costs, which to Marx is a small fraction of the total. In primitive societies, the surplus (profit) goes back to the laborers and to Marx that is fair and just. This naturally assumes that bourgeoisie profits were obscenely large, relative to the pittance paid to laborers.

Today, the average corporate profit margin in the United States is about 9%, or nine cents on every dollar. In most cases this nine cents is either reinvested in the company or paid in dividends as a return on the stockholder's investment. Companies in the growth phase of their life cycle typically reinvest profits back into their companies. The reinvestment of profit for business expansion is critical to the process of new job creation and lower unemployment rates. Mature companies, whose sales have plateaued, typically distribute profits to their stockholders or invest in smaller high-growth businesses. Most dividends distributed by corporations provide a steady flow of supplemental income to retirees.

Marxist Communism

When we think of communism, it is Karl Marx and Friedrich Engels' *(1820-1895)* book *The Communist Manifesto (1848)* that comes to mind. They argue that the history of the world has been one long struggle between the oppressors and the oppressed. In their view, private property was the root of this conflict: property owners were those who owned the businesses that hired the workers; who were then forced through economic necessity to work long, brutal hours for a pittance in wages, never able to earn enough to own land or anything more than the bare necessities of life. The oppressors were those who controlled the means of production, the *Bourgeoisie* (today we would call them capitalists), and those who were oppressed, the *Proletariat* (workers). Marx and Engels advocated and predicted the downfall of the rich bourgeoisie, along with the Parliamentarians (government officials) that protected their wealth, and wrote laws that kept the proletariat overworked, impoverished, and dependent upon the bourgeoisie for a meager existence. It is important to note that the book was written in the mid-19th century, at a time when the Industrial Revolution was in its infancy. In fact, wages were low, working conditions harsh and the hours long. In any case, Marx and Engels believed that the oppression of workers to be a necessary step in the progression of history that would lead to the uprising of workers against their oppressors.

To Marx, socialism was a logical step in the march toward what he considered pure communism, similar in theory to the song *Imagine* by John Lennon. In Marxist Socialism, the government steps in to represent the interests of the workers, as opposed to representing the interests of the bourgeoisie, by gradually enacting policies that restrict and eventually eliminate private property rights, particularly the means of production. In theory, this will be accomplished when the government has complete control over all corporations. This will be accomplished through heavy-handed regulations, and increasingly oppressive taxation on corporations, the wealthy, and inheritance. Eventually all industry and agriculture will be nationalized and everyone will essentially work for the government. There will be no rich or poor, and therefore all class antagonism will disappear. This, however, cannot be accomplished without completely dismantling all existing governmental and commercial structures, and establishing a completely new, (and at the time untested) alternative society. Also, as Marx stated in his book *The Communist Manifesto*, this was not intended to be a nationalist movement, but eventually a worldwide revolution. Thus, "... the Communists everywhere support every revolutionary movement against the existing social and political order of things."

> When class distinctions have disappeared, public power will lose its political character. This is because political power is nothing more than 'the organized power of one class for oppressing another.' When the proletariat eliminate the old conditions for production, they will render class antagonism impossible, and thereby eliminate their own class supremacy. Bourgeois society will be replaced by an 'association' in which 'the free development of each is the condition for the free development of all' [1].

Total Power

Let's pretend that you are a criminal mastermind with an obsession to become the absolute ruler of your country. Unfortunately, you were not born into royalty, great wealth, or a powerful political/ military family. However, you learn about Marxist Socialism. The ideology of a worker-dominated government appeals to the masses, and the nationalization of assets appeals to your greed. You see, if you are the head of the government and the government owns and/or controls everything in the country, then you are absolutely powerful, absolutely corrupt, and immensely wealthy. So, all you have to do is get everyone riled-up, foment a revolution, and completely dismantle all existing institutions. An unfortunate byproduct is the killing or squashing of all opposition; and probably even the true believers, those suckers who actually believed in a communist utopia.

Nationalizing private property means that the state would own your house, your employment, your church (there would be no freedom of religion), and your business. In exchange the state would provide you with a job and all your basic needs. Obviously, this would require a massive despotic taking of everything that you and your countrymen own. Of course, Marx put a positive spin on the process. *The Communist Manifesto* ends with this rallying cry: "Let the ruling classes tremble at a Communist revolution. The proletarians have nothing to lose but their chains. They have a world to win. WORKING MEN OF ALL COUNTRIES, UNITE!"

Historical Communism

Marx's communist utopia has yet to be realized. Even though we refer to them as *Communist*, countries like North Korea, Cuba, Venezuela, and the former Soviet Union all stalled in an advanced state of socialism. With the rise in Marxist Socialism also came the rise of atheism as an alternative to religion. This brought persecution, death, and confiscation of church property. Limited religious freedom was, however, tolerated; in fact, a Soviet Zion (the Jewish Autonomous Oblast) was established in Eastern Russia for Jews in an effort by Joseph Stalin *(1878-1953)* to displace them from mainstream Russian life. As throughout history, if you found yourself on the wrong side of the prevailing orthodoxy, you felt the intense pressure to conform, escape or else be constantly looking over your shoulder.

The historical reality is that the working poor have suffered far more under Marxist Socialism than under the bourgeoisie. In less than 100 years over 90 million people have died either directly or indirectly as a result of Marxist Socialism, be it from civil wars, oppression, or famines caused by authoritarian dictators [2]. Most of the dead were peasants, the people most hopeful that the dream of communism would improve their lives. After all, it was in the poorest countries where Marxist Socialism took root. Marx's followers were not successful in overthrowing the governments of Western Europe or the United States; however, various degrees of *Democratic Socialism* have become embedded in all modern nations. Most of these socialist programs today fall under what Marx would have called *Conservative Socialism*. This is a system where the workers are, according to Marx, temporarily placated by government policies that reduce the influence of capitalism through regulations, minimum wage laws, government supported unions, anti-poverty programs, public education, public healthcare, etcetera. In spite of Marx's criticism of it, some Conservative Socialism has proven to be worthwhile and valuable to society. On the other hand, some can be detrimental to a nation's prosperity.

Minimum Wage Laws

A government-guaranteed minimum wage is an appealing concept. After all, who doesn't want a raise, especially if you are at the bottom of the wage scale? Unions are always advocating for minimum wage increases, and why not? If the bottom tier of workers gets an automatic raise, then increased wages will inevitably flow to all workers. This is because you can't have the bottom tier of workers making more than the next to the bottom tier, and then the next to the bottom tier shouldn't be making more than the next higher level, and so on. Therefore, all union members get a raise as mandated by law! Profits to the greedy bourgeoisie shrink by the same margin that wages increase to the proletariat as a zero-sum gain. Payroll expenses increase without a corresponding increase in labor productivity. So, labor doesn't have to work any harder or longer or more efficiently, they are just given more money. Why? Because the unions and affected workers lobbied Congress and state legislatures. They picketed, gave speeches and held parades, anything to get on the evening news. They hoped that the American people would get behind the idea: "poor underpaid workers deserve to earn a living wage."

The force of law is a powerful tool that can be used by society to deter bad behavior, encourage good behavior and fund the functioning of government, including national defense and law enforcement. But we should remember that the force of law is only one tool, a hammer.

If, for example a minimum wage is established by law, then every employer must pay their employees at least that minimum rate, regardless if the business can afford to make payroll or whether a particular employee is worth the minimum rate to his employer.

It doesn't matter to lawmakers that the increased payroll expense will force many businesses to raise prices and that the subsequent loss of customers will cause some businesses to fail. Lawmakers will feel no responsibility because they were only responding to the demands of voters... Or were they responding to the demands made by labor unions and special interest groups that make up an extremely vocal minority of affected workers. We should remember that legally-mandated regulations like minimum wage laws represent a shift in wealth from employers and consumers to the worker class, which is consistent with Marxist Socialism, but inconsistent with value-based free trade.

There is currently a movement that says $15 per hour is necessary for workers to earn a "Living Wage." And many politicians, including some prominent economists, agree. But, what is a Living Wage for a 19-year-old living at home? Or a 23-year-old sharing an apartment with a friend? Or a retiree working to earn some extra income? Or a single mom with five children all living at home? Or the primary breadwinner supporting a family of four? Obviously, each situation is different and unique.

Productivity

Some would say that slogans such as: "A fair day's wage for a fair day's work" and "Average productivity equals 100% efficiency" are overly-generalized and outmoded ideas. I have heard economists suggest that instead of paying people a minimum wage, or a standard scale, or a rate based on seniority, pay them instead on productivity or how much added value they provide to their employers and customers over and above normal standards of performance. Some examples would include: cost savings ideas, quality improvements, more efficient methods of accomplishing the same task, training; and the sharing of job experience for the benefit of new employees. There is no incentive for the employee if all these activities are lumped together, typed into a job description and then made automatic performance requirements.

There is still the need for a set of minimum job performance expectations, with a commensurate salary and a starting point for new employees. However, it is assumed that companies are smart enough to hire and promote qualified workers and that companies also provide positive work environments, including the proper tools and training to not only attain minimum work standards, but to perform to the best of their employee's abilities. Creative Destruction is not only related to products and processes, it is also related to the management of people and sometimes even to the business models upon which companies are built. If the old models don't work anymore, then replace them with models that do work.

Finally, the drive by corporate America to slash payrolls is not necessarily good for the bottom line. Sometimes more employees, rather than fewer, can make good business sense; but only when they add more value to their customers and employers than their cost.

Unions

I would like to preface my criticisms of labor unions by saying that it is my belief that publicly held companies should, by law, be subject to the unionization of all employees. This is due to varying degrees of worker exploitation, even today, by big companies. Collective Bargaining would tend to keep these companies honest and fair in regard to wages, working conditions, work hours, management expectations and decisions that affect workers. With that being said, union lobbying has had a tremendous, and mostly negative, influence on labor law policies enacted by both the federal and state governments. The result has been a hodgepodge of laws that were written to benefit union employees over the rest of the workforce.

Part of every union member's dues pay for lobbying, and this is where Marxist philosophy comes in. If you remember, under Marxist Socialism, the government steps in to represent the interests of the workers as opposed to representing the interests of the bourgeoisie. And this is exactly what the big unions attempt to do; that is, influence legislation to benefit union members and weaken corporations (the bourgeoisie). However, I said union members, not workers in general. After all, the unions are only representing the interests of their members. I'll use the example of *Exempt* (salaried) and *Non-exempt* (hourly) employees. Exempt meaning that employees have been exempted from inclusion in the *Fair Labor Standards Act*. In other words, a salaried employee can be told to work as many hours as the job requires -- or at the whim of his/her boss -- without the benefit of overtime pay (1.5 times the hourly rate for every hour worked over 40 in any given work week) or, in fact, any compensation over the employee's base salary.

To determine if an employee is exempt or non-exempt is so abstruse that it takes the interpretation of a labor law attorney to advise which classes of employees are to be exempted and which are not; and of course, smart lawyers can take the same class of employees and switch them back and forth depending on which happens to be the cheapest alternative for the company. The law was written to benefit union workers; therefore, the provisions were written in a way that covered most unionized employees, everyone else was classified as salaried (Exempt).

The summer after graduation from college, I took a job in a factory that was unionized. My hours were the standard 40 hours per week and I was required to punch a time clock. At the end of the summer, the company offered me a job in production planning, with a small increase in my rate of pay. In this capacity, however, I was considered salaried and as such exempted from the *Fair Labor Standards Act*. Within a week of starting the job, I was told to work a double shift (sixteen hours); then when Friday came, I was told to work half a day on Saturday. The pattern of double shifts once or twice a week, and four hour Saturdays continued through the fall. Keep in mind that the company, not only didn't have to pay me time and a half, they didn't have to pay me anything over my normal salary. I never bothered to calculate my true hourly rate; it would have been too depressing.

Several years later I accepted a salaried position with a company in a completely different industry. Throughout a period of high company sales growth, we were required to work well over 40 hours per week. The hourly workers sitting next to us, working the same hours, had higher gross earnings than those of us who were salaried, even though their jobs were at a lower pay grade. As salaried employees, however, we were given an extra week of vacation. Some years later when sales were in decline and several of my peers were being laid-off, the company no longer wanted to pay employees for an extra week of vacation -- and since there was very little need for overtime -- the company simply reclassified us as hourly workers. Even though our job titles, offices and responsibilities were the same -- management simply gamed the labor law system.

It is generally true that union representation restrains management from the blatant exploitation of workers. As with other special interests, however, unions have had too much influence over legislation; and labor union strikes can be interpreted as a form of corporate blackmail that often leaves both the workers and the company poorer. They may play into the Marxist desire to destroy capitalist structures, but it's easy to forget that labor and management all work for the same company and the same customers. Any action taken by union members that weaken the company (in this case by shifting customer dollars to a competitor) ultimately weakens their own job security. Instead, binding arbitration can be a fair and efficient method to settle unresolved disputes with management.

In any case, common sense dictates that labor laws should be written to equally protect all workers, not just those with certain job categories or certain job activities.

Managing the Effects of Creative Destruction

A major concern in the United States relates to displaced workers. Lost jobs from plant or mine closings due to trade, technology or dying industries, are not the fault of the workers; and many states simply lack the money to properly support workers who, through creative destruction, are hurt financially.

The idea of government intervention designed to prevent or delay the natural progress of free enterprise -- for the purpose of saving jobs -- is anti-growth and anti-prosperity. In the end it costs society, including workers, more than if a non-interventionist government policy would have been in place.

There are other ways to solve this problem that have their roots in Conservative Socialism; for example, a special-purpose increase in the federal payroll tax could act as an insurance policy/safety net. First, temporarily displaced workers could qualify for an extension of unemployment insurance; second, workers who possess marketable skills, but do not live within commuting distance to a new job could qualify for relocation assistance; third, the government could provide education and training for workers whose skills are now obsolete; and finally, wage adjustment insurance could take effect for workers forced to take a lower-paying job, offsetting a portion of the difference in wages. For example: in the first year, it might make up 75% of prior earnings, in the second year, 50%, in the third year 25%.

Is True Communism Realistic?

Ironically, China and Russia, the former cradles of Marxist Socialism, have both abandoned Marxism to pursue more capitalistic policies, while maintaining totalitarian control of their countries. So much for Marx's ultimate conclusion that communism would result in the abandonment of governments and people would form free communal associations. A flaw in Marxist thinking is that once power in any government is established, those in power will fight to stay in control.

In every major country there is a bureaucracy that numbers in the hundreds of thousands and in the case of the United States, millions. These are all government employees who believe that they are performing vital functions for the betterment of the public, and of course they will jealously guard their livelihoods. Those in leadership have even more to lose if the status quo changes. Therefore, there is a tendency for all governments to pass laws that increase and consolidate their power and wealth, which can effectively decrease individual rights and true national wealth.

A second flaw is the idea that the world would someday become one large classless society. It simply defies human nature. People organize naturally, but there must be meaning, identification, and a sense of belonging for the members or the group collapses. The ideology of a worldwide worker collective holds virtually no meaning or feelings of belonging for anyone. On the other hand, if the whole world was controlled by one universal communist government with one political party, and we all were commanded by law to be one collective, then that would be that. However, aside from the fact that maintaining control of the whole world would be a logistical and police nightmare, collectives by coercion are still contrary to human nature and will ultimately fail.

The third flaw is the historical fact that as an economic system Marxist Socialism has repeatedly failed. In the Soviet Union, North Korea, China, Cuba, Venezuela and elsewhere, economic activity has lagged far behind private capital-based countries. Since the gradual implementation of free market policies, China has soared economically. Cuba, North Korea and Venezuela on the other hand are hold-outs and have suffered greatly from the policies of backward totalitarian regimes. We should remember that mutually beneficial trade is the goose that lays golden eggs and whenever a government kills the goose, then wealth will simply dry up.

Venezuela

In terms of natural resources, one of the richest countries in the world is Venezuela. According to the CIA's *World Factbook*, it has the largest proven oil reserves on earth, estimated at 297 billion barrels. However, its economy has been mismanaged for decades under authoritarian socialism. First by the deceased Hugo Chavez *(1954-2013)*, and now by his successor Nicolas Maduro *(1962-)*. Their oil industry is so corrupt and inefficient that according to an article by the *New York Times*, they recently have been forced to import oil from the United States.

The Venezuelan economy shrank 18% in 2016, according to *CNN Money*; and according to the International Monetary Fund (IMF) inflation is running at about 720%. By the end of 2016, the 100 Bolivar Note was worth about 2 cents.

It wasn't that long ago that Venezuela was a major oil exporter with revenues paying for extensive social programs. The country had officially abandoned capitalism. It was bringing in so much oil money that corruption and the inefficient management of resources was barely noticed. Both, however, were gradually spreading like a virus and pretty soon oil rigs were left abandoned for lack of parts. Thieves were stripping equipment and selling their loot on the black market. Poverty was growing at an alarming rate; and then, with a global drop in the price of oil, the country is now at the brink of disintegration.

Working under Communism

There are basically two different forms of government in the world today: those countries where citizens work for the government, and those countries where the government works for its citizens. In the first example, the government owns or controls the means of production, banking and all commerce. Everyone in the country, who is employed, essentially works for the government. The government decides how much you will earn, how much you will be taxed and how much you will get to keep from your paycheck. It controls what products and services are available and how much they will cost; it also determines what products can be imported from abroad. It owns, controls, and profits from all natural-resources and productive activities within its borders. This system requires an incredibly large -- and typically inadequate -- bureaucracy to manage such a large and complicated enterprise, including the care of all its citizens. These bureaucratic planners can never have enough information to effectively manage the allocation and distribution of resources to broad and diverse populations.

International Trade

Remember that governments have the power of law. The police
and military are always in the background to enforce whatever
laws the government dictates. Therefore, it can force its citizens
to purchase only domestically made products. When the country
enters the international marketplace, however, the rules change. If it
wishes to export finished goods abroad, then it's products must be
internationally competitive. In other words, the products need to fill
a niche in the international market place, be competitively priced,
and provide the quality that international consumers demand.

Of course, even if the country does not export finished goods
and is blessed with an abundance of natural resources, it can always
export raw materials like coal, iron ore, bauxite or oil. Money from
the sale of these commodities can be used to pay for the imports of
goods needed domestically. Russia is a good example; their economy
is dependent on the international demand for its raw materials,
particularly oil. Even though Russia can somewhat control supply
and demand within its own borders, it has no control over the global
price of oil. Because oil is a commodity, Russian oil is worth the same
as oil shipped from any other country. They may have a distribution
advantage relative to certain markets and a disadvantage to others;
but in either case their revenues from exports are dependent on
internationally set oil prices. Great when oil prices are high, but
economically crushing when they are low.

National Wealth

So, where is the wealth of the country concentrated? Does the
government keep its citizens in near poverty while a select few are
allowed to earn massive riches? Does the government allow foreign
investment? Is it politically stable? Does it allow its citizens to keep
enough of their pay to live in a nice home, own an automobile, build
a savings account, and invest for the future?

Authoritarian regimes greatly limit the ability of their countries to build national wealth by concentrating power and money in the hands of a small minority of supporters, and by placing restrictions on foreign investment and international trade. They apparently do not realize that as imports and exports in a country grow, so does the wealth that is flowing into the country.

They could increase national income by allowing citizens to own property, invest in businesses, earn wages based on marketable skills, and build individual wealth. The more citizens there are in countries that have purchasing power, the greater will be the national wealth. The greater the national wealth, the more stable the government and the more the government will collect in taxes to fund public services.

Governments as public entities should operate similarly to private sector companies, because they are both in existence to provide services. Private sector firms must provide more value than their price. Therefore, government services should also provide more value to citizens than they cost -- as determined by consumers, not bureaucrats. So, if you accept this premise, then there is no limit to the size of government other than its ability to continue providing services that add more value to society than their costs to society.

Purchasing Power

Let's look at the country of China. It has a population of well over a billion people, but until recent decades most imports were banned by its government. The economy was largely agrarian and the citizens were poor. As a result, China was ignored by the world as a trading partner. There is a difference between a nation's population and the purchasing power of its citizens.

Today, China is a country that for the past two decades has fueled world economic growth. Domestic and international companies are investing in world class manufacturing facilities, hiring workers and paying ever increasing wages. A growing percentage of the population is achieving middle class. As more of the population achieves wealth, so does the nation.

CHAPTER THREE

Progressivism: Is Big Government Your Friend?

*It is common sense to take a method and try it. If it fails, admit
it frankly and try another. But above all, try something.*
Franklin D. Roosevelt

CEO's love to talk about the free enterprise system and the competitive spirit that built America. They preach less government interference in the private sector, meaning less regulation and red tape -- unless, that is, they are lobbying Congress for tax breaks, or tariff protections, or corporate subsidies, or assistance with opening foreign markets, or corporate bailouts; then government interference is more than welcome, it is demanded.

Consumers love competition, businesses hate it. In fact, every company strives to achieve a monopoly in their chosen market niche. Therefore, some businessmen will use every available trick to unfairly reduce or eliminate competition, including: political arm twisting, acquiring and absorbing smaller, more innovative companies -- or, combining forces with their major competitors to share control of the market by rigging prices, driving smaller companies out of business and carving up markets. The latter, called *Trusts*, ruled the private economy in the years leading up to the 20th Century.

In the late nineteenth century, *Robber Barons* controlled several key industries. A few of the most notables included: Andrew Carnegie *(1835-1919)* (Steel); John D. Rockefeller *(1839-1937)* (Oil); and John

Pierpont Morgan Sr., more commonly known as J.P. Morgan *(1837-1913)* (Banking). By 1904, some 318 trusts controlled almost half of the nation's industrial output. These trusts were very unpopular and the political pushback came from a new movement called *Progressivism*.

While Republican President William McKinley *(1843-1901)* started the ball rolling, it was his Progressive Vice President and successor, Teddy Roosevelt *(1858-1919)*, that made "Trust Busting" famous. Roosevelt's *Square Deal* had three components: conservation of natural resources, control of corporations, and consumer protection. He used the Interstate Commerce Commission to curb monopolistic pricing by the railroads and to improve safety; he used the *Sherman Antitrust Act* to break up the Beef Trust; he pushed Congress to pass the *Pure Food and Drug Act*; and he established the Departments of Commerce and Labor. Standard Oil, which at its peak controlled nearly 90% of the country's oil production, was eventually broken up by the Supreme Court.

The Progressive movement was also instrumental in cleaning up political corruption at the local level, particularly in big cities. This problem evolved from the rise of immigrants, many of whom had no jobs, no political clout, and who lived huddled in the slums of major cities. Political bosses, many of whom had their roots in the slums, found these groups to be ripe sources of votes. Sometimes in conjunction with organized crime, jobs were obtained, judges paid-off, and charity was given to those in need. There was the expectation that if you received a favor, then you would spread the word and support your benefactors. As you might expect, this system was very unpopular with the squeaky-clean Progressive reformers.

Over the next few decades, Progressives evolved to believe that the militarization of a planned society was the most efficient means for a nation to allocate resources, control corporations, and eliminate all the negative aspects of society without the messy and confining constraints of a democracy.

The Progressive movement became comfortable with the idea that the federal government should either control businesses through tight regulations or replace capitalism entirely with public investment;

and that a strong progressive leader should be given free rein to fix every national problem and lead the world internationally. In other words, Progressivism could solve any problem through the strong leadership of a Progressive President and his centralized Washington bureaucracy. Many Progressives in the intelligentsia believed that the United States should adopt a less democratic, more autocratic government. Fascist and Marxist ideologies became popular Progressive alternatives to our cumbersome separation of powers. By the 1930's many Progressives favored a Fascist-style President to save us from the Great Depression. This mentality led to the immense power of the Neo-progressive, Franklin Delano Roosevelt *(1882-1945)*.

The new progressives, like FDR believed that the masses should be used like tools; enticed by the wise and patriarchal leader to bend to his will and his perception of what was best for the organic, collective whole. To this end, the leader would attempt to unify the masses with the power of nationalistic rhetoric to stir emotions and patriotism, thus bypassing any rational democratic debate. The same goals could be achieved by exploiting national emergencies, such as war or an economic depression. These neo-progressives were frustrated by the constraints of their political structures and believed that they should be free to enact any law by decree [1].

Unlike Marxist Socialism, the Progressive government was not necessarily interested in representing the interests of the proletariat. The government was to become an end in itself, representing neither the bourgeoisie nor the proletariat, but its own interests. Rather than the internationalist "Workers of the World Unite," nationalism became the unifying concept. In retrospect, however, FDR's bold experimentation followed a path that looked more like Stalinism, where the leadership wanted everyone dependent on the State -- for the purposes of control and consolidation of power.

Franklin Delano Roosevelt

Franklin wanted very much to be loved and revered by the people. His aristocratic upbringing gave him a sense of entitlement and a feeling that he was a step above other people: better and wiser. On the one hand, he was a cruel, calculating politician who could manoeuver any situation to his advantage. On the other, his public persona was that of a kind patriarch, complemented by a powerful, but soothing voice, which he used very effectively in his speeches and famous "Fireside Chats." Millions listened intently to his every word, broadcast by radio over the entire country. He would actively listen to his advisors and visitors, and upon leaving they would believe that Franklin was in agreement with their positions. However, he was actually just being agreeable, but non-committal. Once he had made up his own mind on a course of action, he shut out dissent -- and unless you wanted to suffer his wrath, you kept your mouth shut and went along.

He believed that his presidency should be for life: Franklin was fifty-one years old when he assumed the Presidency and died twelve years later while still in office -- after winning four consecutive four-year terms -- apparently, he convinced the country that he was right.

His *New Deal* is widely heralded by liberal historians and Democrats as bold experimentation that shortened the Great Depression; gave jobs to millions of unemployed workers; completed many useful infrastructure projects; and perhaps most importantly, infused much needed hope to a suffering nation:

> *And the truth is, it will take more than a few years for us to solve challenges that have built up over decades. It will require common effort, shared responsibility, and the kind of bold, persistent experimentation that Franklin Roosevelt pursued during the only crisis worse than this one.*
>
> *Barak Obama, 2012 acceptance speech for his party's nomination to the Presidency. Charlotte, North Carolina*

The Great Depression

It is understandable that this assessment would come from a modern progressive like former President Obama. But are quotes like this liberal mythology or an accurate assessment of his tenure in office? To properly understand the New Deal, it is important to first look at the causes behind the *Great Depression*. In March of 1929 the economy started to weaken, which was a jolt because it had been sailing along through most of the 1920's under the fiscally conservative President, Calvin Coolidge *(1872-1933)*. During the Roaring 20's, the stock market had been rising higher and higher. It seemed like such a sure thing that people from all walks of life were borrowing money to invest in the stock market, often buying stocks with only a 10% cash investment, the other 90% was a loan against the stock. Even banks were pouring their depositor's money into the market. Back then there was no *Securities and Exchange Commission* or limits on stock market investments by U.S. banks. With absolutely no government regulation, big-money players were able to manipulate the stock prices of many corporations. It didn't seem as though anybody was actually paying attention to the underlying value of stocks being purchased -- they were all going up, up, up, so who cared? Well, they should have, because a market bubble was inadvertently being created and it was about to burst.

The market did collapse in October of 1929, partly due to the weakening economy and partly due to a huge new tariff bill being discussed in Congress. Wall Street suspected that this sweeping bill, affecting some 20,000 imported products, would incite a trade war, weakening U.S. corporations. Perhaps most importantly, the market was simply stretched to the breaking point. The prices of stocks became so out of line with profits that their underlying values could no longer justify new buyers, even under the **Greater Fool Theory**. Then, the *Smoot-Hawley Tariff* was passed on June 17 of 1930 and immediately deepened the recession. Thereafter, Congress passed the *Revenue Act of 1932*, which significantly raised taxes across the board. And finally, when it seemed that matters couldn't get worse, the Federal Reserve reacted to the banking crisis by tightening the money supply.

Part of the Federal Reserve's logic had nothing to do with the worsening economy. When Roosevelt took office, the United States was on the gold standard. This meant that a lowering of interest rates would create a greater demand for the cheaper dollars, leading to an increase in our nation's money supply -- which would require the treasury to purchase additional gold to cover the newly printed currency. Therefore, by raising interest rates, less money was printed. The Federal Reserve Board's decision not only decreased the need to purchase gold, but the treasury could actually sell off some of the gold that was stored in Fort Knox. However, the decreased liquidity meant that the banks had no money to lend -- especially after the "run" on banks by worried depositors who had lost faith in the banking system.

Let's review this perfect storm of private and public-sector ineptitude.

- Investors foolishly assumed that the market would continue to rise forever, ignoring the underlying value of the stocks in the exchange.
- Banks were using depositor's hard-earned money to also speculate in the Stock Market. After the stock market crashed, banks experienced a huge decrease in the value of their stock holdings, causing serious losses and decreased liquidity.
- Investors were using highly leveraged money to speculate in the Stock Market.
- The Federal Reserve tightened the money supply, exacerbating the liquidity crises: bank failures multiplied, customers panicked and demanded their money from banks, which further decreased bank liquidity and resulted in more bank failures.

There were almost 25,000 commercial banks in the summer of 1929, by early 1933 that

*number was down to about 15,000. During
the same time period bank deposits shrank
by over a third* [2].

- Because Congress was angry at European countries for not paying their World War I war debts and reparation payments, they passed the punitive *Smoot-Hawley Tariff* to force money from the welchers. This, of course, instigated retaliation and the ensuing trade war deepened the recession into the Great Depression.
- Five months before FDR took office, Congress passed the *Revenue Act of 1932* which raised taxes across the board. The top tax rate went from 25% to 63%. The estate tax was doubled and corporate taxes were raised by 15%. These tax increases both hurt the economy and killed any chance at recovery.

Publicly traded corporations were no longer able to raise capital in the stock market. Then because of the liquidity crises, banks had no money to lend. To make matters worse, foreign trade dropped 70%, which meant that manufacturers faced supply shortages, and foreign markets dried-up causing exports to dwindle. People were losing their jobs in droves, banks didn't have any money to lend, and corporations were suffering huge losses. What I have just described is the mess that FDR inherited!

It should be mentioned that not every investor was inept. Joseph Kennedy *(1888-1969)* made millions during the boom and then foreseeing the bust, took all his money out of the market. Another savvy investor, Jesse Livermore *(1877-1940)* made millions going "long" during the market's rise and then switched to "short" positions at its peak; thus, making millions more during its massive decline.

It is interesting that progressive revisionists have used the Great Depression as proof that capitalism can never be a viable economic system, and that only a progressive government is truly capable of managing the economy; however, even with the mistakes made in the private sector, the Great Depression would have been a minor historical event if it wasn't for the incredible blunders made by Congress, the Federal Reserve, and Presidents Hoover and Roosevelt.

There were some steps that could have been taken to correct these blunders: First, FDR could have put pressure on Congress to repeal *Smoot-Hawley* and then reduced tariffs below their previous levels. He then could have put pressure on our trading partners to reduce their tariffs. Next, he could have convinced the Federal Reserve to immediately increase the nation's money supply. Then they could have infused money into the banking system. Many viable banks failed simply due to a lack of liquidity caused by the Federal Reserve. (Whether you are in favor of bank bailouts or not, it is critical that a nation's banking system is stable and inspires domestic and international confidence.) Finally, FDR could have pushed Congress to completely repeal Hoover's *Revenue Act of 1932*.

These steps would have dramatically shortened the Great Depression. By eliminating it's causes what remained would have been a routine business cycle recession -- FDR took none of these actions.

What FDR Did Right

FDR's establishment of the *Federal Deposit Insurance Corporation* (FDIC), which insures depositors against the possibility of a bank failure, was a good step in reestablishing bank confidence. He then cleaned up investor fraud and separated the securities industry from commercial banking, which he accomplished with passage of the *Securities and Exchange Act*, establishing the *Securities and Exchange Commission* (SEC), and the *Glass-Steagall Act* which created a distinct separation between investment banking and commercial banking.

From a philosophical standpoint, the old system was justifiable. Before the FDIC, if a bank made bad investments, bad loans, or was poorly managed, the free-market would theoretically intervene. Disappointed investors would sell their stock, lowering the market value of the bank. Depositors would take their money elsewhere and the bank would be forced to improve or go out of business. In a worst-case scenario, those investors and depositors still hanging on would lose their money, which was a risk that they voluntarily took.

The problems with the old system, however, were transparency and sophistication. Banks that were privately owned did not have a responsibility to share the bank's financial statements with the public, and even those financial statements made available by publicly traded banks were of little value to most depositors. This is because, to the average person, bank financial statements are practically unintelligible. Plus, they require time and research, something very few depositors would bother to do.

FDR wanted a system where anyone could walk into any bank in the country with absolute confidence that their deposits were 100% secure. To this end, he came up with an ingenious solution: mandate by law that all banks must pay premiums to a federally-backed insurance company, the FDIC. Therefore, the banking system itself paid, through insurance premiums, for its own stability. On the door of the bank, customers could look at a sign that said: "This Institution is Backed by the Full Faith and Credit of the United States." No more runs on banks by angry and fearful customers, draining the vaults of much needed liquidity.

For the government to be willing to back the banking industry, however, there was needed a greater degree of scrutiny on banking activities. It was this concern that led to Glass-Steagall and the requirement that banks "stick to their own knitting," so to speak.

My primary criticism is in regard to Roosevelt's motives. As you will soon see, there is substantial evidence to suggest that FDR was more interested in enhancing his own power than returning the country to prosperity. In fact, it is possible that he learned a valuable lesson from Woodrow Wilson *(1856-1924)*. During World War I. Wilson was granted almost authoritarian, emergency war time powers, however, after the war ended, those powers were removed by Congress, over his objections. In Roosevelt's inaugural address he stated

I shall ask the Congress for the one remaining instrument to meet the crises - broad Executive

power to wage a war against the emergency, as great
as the power that would be given me if we were in fact
invaded by a foreign foe...

I wouldn't be surprised if FDR believed that the longer he kept the country in crisis, the longer he would be able to maintain the country's dependence on him. Regardless of his intentions, however, his policies did lengthen the Depression. See the chart below:

Depression Era Unemployment Statistics

Year	Population	Labor Force	Unemployed	Percentage of Labor Force Unemployed
1929	88,010,000	49,440,000	1,550,000	3.14
1930	89,550,000	50,080,000	4,340,000	8.67
1931	90,710,000	50,680,000	8,020,000	15.82
1932	91,810,000	51,250,000	12,060,000	23.53
1933	92,950,000	51,840,000	12,830,000	24.75
1934	94,190,000	52,490,000	11,340,000	21.60
1935	95,460,000	53,140,000	10,610,000	19.97
1936	96,700,000	53,740,000	9,030,000	16.80
1937	97,870,000	54,320,000	7,700,000	14.18
1938	99,120,000	54,950,000	10,390,000	18.91
1939	100,360,000	55,600,000	9,480,000	17.05
1940	101,560,000	56,180,000	8,120,000	14.45
1941	102,700,000	57,530,000	5,560,000	9.66

Source: http://www.u-s-history.com/pages/h1528.html

Let's give FDR the benefit of the doubt and assume that his *New Deal* needed a few years to take effect. So, if we just look at the unemployment rate for his second term, it still averages over 16%! By comparison, the unemployment rate during the *Great Recession* that began in 2008 topped out at 9.6%.

Also, consider that the U.S. unemployment rate in 1938 (five years after taking office) compared to the rest of the world was also dismal. Of the sixteen countries surveyed by the League of Nations, we were in thirteenth place. Only three of the sixteen countries had higher unemployment rates. Ours was almost double that of the average world index. (As a side note, the reduction in unemployment from 1940 to 1941 was directly related to a huge increase in defense related contracts, as FDR ramped-up military spending from $2.2 billion in 1940 to a whopping $7.2 billion in 1941.)

Gold and Silver

As you may recall, when FDR took office the United States was on the Gold Standard, meaning that in addition to the "Full Faith and Credit of the United States," our nation's currency was backed by gold; and as a check against inflation, the price, for the past thirty years had been set at $20.67 an ounce. Roosevelt's "Brain Trust" (mostly academics from Columbia University) incorrectly believed that if they raised the price of gold, inflation would occur. Farmers and businessmen would therefore be able to sell their products at higher prices.

In addition, FDR knew that his administration was going to be throwing around large amounts of money to pay for the New Deal and he also knew that the money would not be completely covered by revenues. He did not want the government to be forced to back all this new currency with gold, so he did two things: first, he took the country off the gold standard, and then he began hoarding gold. Anyone in possession of gold was required by law (and fear of fines and imprisonment) to exchange their gold for currency. He then canceled any government contracts that were to be paid in gold, and started buying gold from mining companies and foreigners. Through the Treasury Department, he was buying up gold from world markets at increasingly higher prices. Meanwhile, the mining companies were loving the increased production and high prices.

In 1934 Congress authorized the *Gold Reserve Act* which fixed the price of gold at $35 an ounce. The federal government now had in its possession 190 million ounces in gold, most of which was purchased at much cheaper prices. And none of it was needed to back the currency! FDR had made a nice profit for the treasury, but it was largely at the expense of his citizens who had been the primary holders of his gold.

The deflation that had occurred as a result of falling prices did not turn around. There was such a weak demand for currency as a result of the Great Depression that Roosevelt's New Deal spending was not enough to compensate for weak private-sector demand. Further, he discovered that while increased gold purchases by the government raised the price of gold, it did nothing to benefit other commodity prices.

Silver miners wanted in on the action. So, at the behest of politicians from the seven "Silver Bloc" States, Roosevelt agreed to pay them 64.5 cents an ounce for all their production, even though the current price of silver was 40 to 45 cents an ounce. Congress then passed the *Silver Purchase Act* in 1934 which allowed for silver purchases up to one-third of the nation's reserve, or the price limit of $1.29 an ounce. Silver production sky-rocketed. The boondoggle lasted for fifteen years and ultimately cost the taxpayers about $1.5 billion (almost $27.5 billion today) [3]. With the signing of this act, Congress and the President had nationalized both the gold and silver industries. And as with gold, he forced his citizens to redeem all silver holdings in exchange for U.S. currency.

As previously mentioned, Roosevelt and his progressive advisors believed that the economic downturn was caused by *Free-market Capitalism*, which they believed to be a failed system. The capitalists were to blame for "overproduction", a situation where too many goods and services are produced relative to their demand. Overproduction leads to deflation, or in other words, falling prices and falling wages. In their minds, the solution was to restrict production which would result in increased prices and wages, thus pulling the economy up and out of the economic depression. As we saw with gold, it was Roosevelt's intention to use the government to control the nation's output of commodities, agricultural, and industrial production, and to limit foreign imports to protect American workers. While

Roosevelt may have believed in this flawed strategy; it appears that his personal ambitions trumped his desire to help a suffering nation. As a side note, it was never Roosevelt's goal to infuse massive amounts of currency into the private sector as Keynes would have advised (more on Keynes later). Roosevelt was not trying to stimulate the private sector; he was trying to replace the private sector with government run programs, as Marx would have advised. But unlike Marx, he was not using government to represent the proletariat; instead he intended to use and control the bourgeoisie to further his own political ambitions. Here are a few examples.

The NRA

One of the first acts of the New Deal was the *National Industrial Recovery Act* (NIRA), later Shortened to the NRA. Industry and labor leaders were invited to Washington to set *Codes of Fair Competition*, which would be binding on all producers, under force of law, including fines and imprisonment. The code would "determine how much a factory could expand, what wages had to be paid, the number of hours worked and the prices of all products sold by industry" [4]. As you might expect, Washington was packed with businessmen who wanted to influence the new law. They wanted high prices that would shut out the competitive advantage by low-cost producers. Labor wanted shorter hours and higher wages. The result was a huge advantage for big business and labor; a huge disadvantage for consumers; and smaller, more efficient and innovative companies. Consumers had to pay more for goods at a time when they were already stretched financially [5]. It also hurt exports, because even though FDR could somewhat control economic activity within the borders of the United States, he could not force other countries to buy our products at artificially inflated prices. Therefore, the NRA hurt our nation's exports. In a nutshell, it was a failure as an economic policy -- and it was unconstitutional. In 1935, the Supreme Court (in *Schechter Poultry Corp. v United States*) voted 9 – 0 to shut it down.

The AAA

Roosevelt's next bold experiment was the *Agricultural Adjustment Act* (AAA). Farmers had been complaining to Congress since the end of World War I (WWI) about low farm prices. Dwindling farm exports, improved fertilizers, new more efficient farm equipment and techniques resulted in the U.S. agricultural capacity outstripping demand. By the 1930's many farmers had moved to the city, leaving only about 30% of the population on the farm. Many of the recently urbanized ex-farmers were now unemployed. The *Smoot-Hawley Tariff*, with the intent of helping farmers, simply caused retaliatory tariffs lowering U.S. farm exports. As a result of the farming crises, Herbert Hoover *(1874-1964)* decided something had to be done. He therefore created the *Federal Farm Board* which took two major crops, wheat and cotton, and arbitrarily pegged 1930's prices to those from a pre-WWI period when farm prices were at historically high levels. So, the most politically powerful growers were able to sell their produce at a federally guaranteed minimum price: $0.80 for a bushel of wheat and $0.20 for a pound of cotton. As a consequence, farmers expanded acreage to take advantage of the new high price guarantee. Growers of other produce suddenly switched from their existing crops to wheat and cotton. The federal government purchased the entire surplus and stored it in newly-built grain elevators. "After about two years of wild overproduction, the government had spent the $500 million allocated to the Farm Board. They stopped the programs and gave away or sold at huge losses about 250 million bushels of wheat and 10 million bales of cotton" [6].

In response to a very well publicized farmer's strike, the *Agriculture Adjustment Act* (AAA) was established as a replacement to Hoover's failed *Federal Farm Board*. Under FDR's new scheme, the overproduction/low-price problem would be solved by paying farmers to -- not farm! In addition to just wheat and cotton growers, everyone in the farming business clamored to be included in this lucrative new program: wheat, cotton, field corn, hogs, rice, tobacco, milk and other dairy products were designated as basic commodities in the original legislation. Subsequent amendments in 1934 and 1935 expanded the list of basic commodities to include rye, flax, barley, grain sorghum, cattle, peanuts, sugar beets, sugar cane, and potatoes. This new boondoggle was paid for by a special tax on the food and textile processors.

The AAA was administered autocratically by the Secretary of Agriculture, who set parity prices for each crop, how much land a farmer could set aside, how much the farmer would be paid, as well as determining the processing tax for millers and textile companies. This massive program was managed by 3,000 county agents and 100,000 men to enforce and administer the acreage requirements.

If you are curious as to how it turned out:

> *The United States had, for almost the first time in its national history, become a major food-importing nation. In 1933, the U.S. was plowing under 10 million acres of cotton and killing 6 million piglets; in 1935, the U.S. was importing 36 million [bales] of cotton and 2 million pounds of ham and bacon. We were also importing other basic commodities – butter, corn and even wheat* [7].

The public outcry against food destruction was so great that in 1933 Roosevelt was forced to take action. He therefore established a quasi-public nonprofit organization called the Federal Surplus Relief Corporation -- to purchase the farmers "overproduction" and distribute the resulting food and textiles to needy families through existing relief programs. By 1935, when the country was starving and suffering under oppressive tax rates, citizens were expected to pay artificially higher prices for their meats, produce, and clothes. Textile companies, millers, and meat packers were laying-off workers and some were going out of business entirely. Meanwhile, the Department of Agriculture was continually tinkering with prices and agricultural production levels causing underproduction in some years and overproduction in others [8].

In 1936, the Supreme Court ruled the program unconstitutional. Undaunted, Roosevelt simply ironed out the legal issues and reestablished the Agency in 1938. This time there was no processors tax. It was just another agency to be included in the federal budget.

The economist Friedrich Hayek *(1899-1992)* believed this type of government planning to be a form of socialist collectivism that would ultimately lead to totalitarianism. He argued that it was impossible for government planners to fully achieve market equilibrium because each individual planner would never have enough information to properly balance the supply and demand of a commodity or product. And that the underlying assumptions upon which decisions were made could potentially be based on incorrect or subjective assumptions. For example, Roosevelt's "Brain Trust" made the incorrect assumption that by raising gold prices, other commodity prices would also rise. Another problem faced by all economic planners is that current decisions are always based on historical data. Because markets are dynamic and ever-changing they will always be behind the curve, never able to maintain equilibrium as effectively as natural market forces. Remember that in a free market, price is the constantly changing tool that keeps supply and demand in equilibrium.

The RA

An unintended consequence of the *Agricultural Adjustment Act* involved tenant farmers who were evicted from lands previously farmed, but now set aside as part of the AAA program. In response to this problem, a new program called the *Resettlement Administration* (RA) was established under the leadership of trusted "Brain Trust" member, Rexford Tugwell *(1891-1979)*. His idea was for the government to purchase cheap land outside of urban population centers, then to build model communities and entice the displaced tenant farmers to move in. Unfortunately, they often couldn't find appropriate work, and when they did they displaced other workers who then became unemployed. The housing units in poverty-stricken West Virginia were built to Eleanor Roosevelt's elaborate specifications, but no one could afford the housing units without government support. The agency also built 95 relief camps in California for poor migrant workers, however, the living quarters were only temporary. In the end, the relatively few families that were aided by the program were not enough to justify its extreme costs and unpopularity in Congress. By 1936 Tugwell was forced out of his job. In addition to its other problems, the District of Columbia U.S. Circuit Court of Appeals ruled that the program was an unconstitutional use of federal power.

The WPA

Throughout the history of the United States charity had been considered a local and mostly private function. That changed under Herbert Hoover and the passage of the *Emergency Relief and Construction Act of 1932*. Congress allocated $300 million to be distributed to the states for relief efforts. This was supposed to be a "needs-based" loan program, and therefore a formula was established as to how the money should be distributed; however, the formula was subjective and some governors were philosophically opposed and rejected the program, while others gamed the system and received most of the money.

Roosevelt continued, and in fact, expanded relief aid to the states, but under the new name: *Federal Emergency Relief Administration* (FERA). FERA was a New Deal government spending program established to give direct cash assistance to the poor. Before long, however, problems started occurring. First, private charity organizations began losing donations. Foundations and private donors were now hesitant to donate. Charity began to be perceived as a function of government. Second, payments to the states were intended to be matching funds. The states would put up a certain amount of money and the federal government would fund the remaining need, however, there was a great deal of discretion built into the program and soon states were crying poor. They claimed to have very little money to meet the matching funds requirement and therefore needed FDR to put up the bulk of the money. Pretty soon he simply used the program to help states that supplied needed electoral support, in favor of those who may have a greater need but could not help FDR politically [8]. Third and perhaps most importantly, people now had an incentive to stop trying. Why even bother to find a job if the government will just give you a hand-out? By 1935, Roosevelt accepted the failure and in that year's State of the Union address he stated: "To dole out relief in this way is to administer a narcotic, a subtle destroyer of the human spirit. It is inimical to the dictates of a sound policy" [9].

Next FDR started a new work relief program called the *Works Progress Administration* (WPA). This program was to allow people the opportunity to retain their dignity and self-respect. They could now work and earn a government pay-check as opposed to relying on charity. In total, the program employed 8.5 million workers. WPA employees built bridges, roads, hospitals, schools, parks, and airports. They also painted buildings and murals and built sculptures. Women were involved in sewing, bookbinding, caring for the elderly, school lunch programs, nursery school, and recreational work. According to Digital History, in its eight years of existence, the program cost taxpayers over $11 billion. Well not exactly, because most of the New Deal expenses were not covered by tax revenues. Instead they were added to the national debt. And yes, that money is still part of today's $20 trillion debt.

To the extent that these jobs added more value to society than their cost, then they were justifiable. However, many of the jobs were essentially worthless: men driving around the county counting caterpillars or throwing up shabbily constructed buildings that had to be torn down and rebuilt. More important was the political capital that Roosevelt gained from controlling the process:

> *Frank Kent* (a journalist, political theorist and critic of the New Deal) *watched this corrupt process firsthand and viewed it as almost inevitable. 'Every city and state needs its portion of this incredible*

great sum.' Kent observed. 'They all want as much as
they can get. Failure to secure its proportion places
a state at great disadvantage. It means heavier local
taxation...' 'Thus mayors and governors 'are obliged
to woo Mr. Roosevelt. They must have the money and
he has it to give'... [10].

As further evidence of his political maneuverings: "Gavin Wright, an economic historian, did a state-by-state analysis of New Deal spending. He noted that safe Democratic states, especially those in the South, received fewer WPA dollars than richer battleground states in the North and West. Since southern states had more poverty than northern states that meant that WPA jobs often went to the states that needed them the least" [11].

We rarely hear the term "patronage" anymore, but without it FDR would not have been able to amass his tremendous political power. Patronage is the practice of rewarding party loyalists with jobs. And while every President has used it for political advantage, none had access to as much money as FDR. His alphabet soup of agencies, principally: AAA, FERA, CCC, and the WPA were not doled out based on need, but through a very sophisticated system of political analysis. The program was run by James Farley *(1888-1976)*, the Chairman of the Republican National Committee. His assistant Emil Hurja *(1892-1953)* was the Deputy Director of the Democratic National Committee. It was their job to make sure that jobs from the above-mentioned agencies best served the Democratic Party -- Hurja was an excellent pollster and political analyst.

These political operatives had the country broken-up state by state, district by district, and county by county. They knew where Democrats were strong and where they were weak. They paid particular attention to the swing states; then they strategically directed federal projects, jobs and dollars where they would do the most good -- for them. They also dangled the prospect of big projects in front of local officials, through targeted surveys, just before elections. A tactic that is still in use today.

Leading up to the 1934 elections, the Democrats faced the prospect of losing seats in both the House and the Senate, which was typical during the mid-term of a first-term President. Roosevelt badly wanted strong Democratic backing for his New Deal agenda and was afraid of losing seats in either house of Congress. So he put Farley and Hurja on the job. Enormous amounts of pre-election money flooded states and Democrat-held Congressional Districts that they believed were vulnerable to Republican gains. Next, they targeted districts where they believed Republicans incumbents were vulnerable. They had an early opportunity in Maine to test their ideas. Maine was the only state to hold their elections in September instead of November. Louis Brann *(1876-1948)*, Maine's recently elected Governor, elected on the heels of Roosevelt's 1932 landslide, took out large ads in key newspapers reminding voters that their Governor had secured $108 million from the federal government, providing 44,000 jobs and boldly asserted that: "The Roosevelt policies are such that a state must have friendly contacts in Washington to properly serve the interests of its people" [12].

The Democrats were successful in Maine so similar tactics were used around the country. The results were astounding: Democrats picked up nine Senate seats and a gain of nine House seats. The new balance of power gave Democrats a total of 319 seats in the House of Representatives; the Republicans only 103. In the Senate, the margin was 69 Democrats to 25 Republicans. As long as FDR could keep his party under thumb, he had complete control of both the executive and the legislative branches of government.

FDR was a master at using the carrot to gain political support. By throwing massive amounts of federal dollars and patronage jobs to New Deal supporters, particularly in swing states, and by denying them to opponents, it behooved every politician in the country to curry his favor and support his New Deal legislation.

Frank Hague *(1876-1956)*, the Democratic mayor of Jersey City illustrates the point. Hague was a corrupt politician, but instrumental in Roosevelt's narrow victory in New Jersey; a critical swing state in the 1932 election. Therefore, Roosevelt directed all WPA patronage jobs in New Jersey through him, almost 100,000 jobs in the 1930's. The workers also enjoyed the highest pay rate in the country; however, they were required to contribute 3% of their salaries to the Democratic Party at election time [13]. Incidentally, the scoundrel was able to skim-off a portion of the WPA salaries for himself!

THE RICH

FDR and his "Brain Trust" incorrectly assumed that if the top marginal tax rate was 79%, the wealthy would pay 79% of their earnings to the federal government to pay for New Deal programs. However, the wealthy, then as now, had high-priced accountants and tax attorneys. Corporations delayed investments in new plants, equipment, and personnel. Individuals scoured the tax code for legal loopholes, such as deductions, exemptions, and tax shelters. If all else failed, they simply moved their investments out of the country and money to off-shore tax havens. Consequently, government revenues were not going up as much as FDR had expected. This infuriated Roosevelt, who considered the scoundrels unpatriotic.

Conversely, Andrew Mellon *(1855-1937)*, the former Treasury Secretary under Calvin Coolidge, believed that in order to maximize revenues to the federal government, the top marginal tax rates should be around 24%. In 1921 the highest marginal rate was 73%. Between 1922 and 1925 rates were gradually lowered by Congress to a low in 1925 of 25%. Under Roosevelt's theory, total federal revenues should have gone down proportionately, but they didn't; they stayed steady at about $4 billion dollars per year (approximately $56 billion in today's dollars) until the Great Depression lowered revenues in 1931.

In spite of bad economic policies, however, revenues did continue to climb throughout Roosevelt's presidency; but unlike Coolidge who maintained a budget surplus each of his four years in office, Roosevelt's budget was continually plastered in red ink -- his spending far outpaced revenues. Between 1933 and 1936, Roosevelts first term in office, total US federal government revenues were $12.484 billion, total expenditures were $25.779 billion creating a cumulative deficit (or in the private sector a loss) of $13.295 billion. In other words, Roosevelt spent more than twice as much money as the federal government brought-in. And by 1940, the end of his second term, that deficit had grown to over $21 billion. Also, FDR couldn't admit that he himself was one of the scoundrels that he publicly besmirched. Hypocritically, he used every loophole and deduction available under the tax code to shelter his own personal income. For example, he took a $9,900 (over $100,000 today) tax deduction for donating books, naval prints and other materials to his own presidential library [14].

What FDR didn't seem to understand was that:

- High tax rates discourage private sector business investment.
- That there is a direct correlation between business investment and business expansion; and that investment money is fluid, it moves from high tax nations to low tax nations; and it moves close to the greatest number of customers and potential economic activity.
- That there is a direct correlation between business expansion and new private sector job creation.
- That this job creation provides economic activity that produces goods and services like food, clothes and shelter.
- And finally, that increased economic activity also increases tax revenues. Additionally, there is a direct correlation between high tax rates and the level of activity in the underground economy or "Black Market." The higher the tax rates, the bigger the Black Market.

If we review FDR's first term in office we find that through patronage and intimidation he controlled both houses of Congress and the nation's Governors. In addition. He silenced vocal New Deal critics, including the press, by selectively and personally directing the IRS to perform exhaustive audits on these individuals. The Justice Department was then directed to aggressively pursue prosecutions that sometimes resulted in financial ruin and even imprisonment.

He had accomplished all this but still did not have control over the third branch of government: The Supreme Court. They dared shoot down as unconstitutional some of his prized New Deal programs and he wanted yes-men not independent judicial thinkers.

He therefore came up with an innovative approach to controlling the court. Today it is known as the "Court Packing Plan," though its official name was the *Judicial Procedures Reform Bill of 1937*. The Constitution did not stipulate that there must be nine justices on the bench; however, Congress did provide in the *Judiciary Act of 1869* that there would be one Chief Justice and eight Associate Justices. So, in FDR's mind, all he had to do was convince Congress to pass his reform act and he could control all three branches of government.

The plan went like this: the President would be allowed to appoint up to six new justices, one for each existing judge who was over the age of seventy and six months but had not yet chosen to retired. As it turned out however, there were limits to Roosevelt's popularity and power over Congress. The bill was ultimately defeated, even though Roosevelt made it the centerpiece of his second term in office. As events unfolded, however, it was Roosevelt's longevity in office that finally gave him the power. Before his death he was able to appoint enough justices to give him the majority he so badly wanted.

By 1942, Roosevelt had his majority on the Supreme Court and the *Agricultural Adjustment Act of 1938* was still in full swing. It was under the auspices of this act that one of the most peculiar Supreme Court decisions in history was made: *Wickard v. Filburn, (Claude R. Wickard, Secretary of Agriculture, et al. v. Roscoe C. Filburn, 317 U.S. 111)*. If you remember, FDR was attempting to drive up farm prices. To that end the Secretary of Agriculture had the authority to set limits on the amount of land that a farmer could use to grow wheat, which he did in the case of Roscoe Filburn. Mr. Filburn was growing more wheat than what was allowed under the program and was therefore ordered to pay a fine. But Roscoe objected on the grounds that he was growing the excess wheat for his own consumption and that of his livestock, and had no intention of selling the excess wheat on the open market.

You might ask: how on earth can it be a federal offense for a farmer to grow wheat on his own land and for his own consumption? Through an incredible stretch of logic that goes like this: The Court decided that Filburn's wheat growing activities reduced the amount of wheat he would buy for chicken feed on the open market, which was traded nationally through interstate commerce. Although Filburn's relatively small amount of wheat above what he was allotted would not affect interstate commerce itself, the cumulative actions of thousands of other farmers just like Filburn would certainly become substantial. Therefore, according to the Supreme Court, Filburn's production could be regulated by the federal government.

This is the court case that opened the floodgates for federal intervention in virtually every aspect of American life. It was the philosophy behind this court case that set the stage for later Presidents to exploit. The size and scope of today's federal government has its roots in *Wickard v. Filburn*, and it's incredibly broad interpretation of interstate commerce.

The Progressive philosophy was exhibited by every action, every program, every agency and every minute of political maneuvering taken by Roosevelt. There was no consideration given to a "Free-market" approach to any of the problems. Businessmen and constituents were treated like children who needed the strong arm of government to tell them what they could and what they could not do. His political power came from money, but it wasn't his money. He took the people's money and then doled it back to them strategically and in a way that made them dependent on him.

Unfortunately, today's progressivism looks more like Franklin Roosevelt's vision than Teddy Roosevelt's. Teddy wanted to protect consumers from the worst tendencies of capitalism. Franklin, on the other hand, wanted control of capitalism to further his own political ambitions. Similarly, today's politicians are following in his Washington-centered footsteps. The power of the executive branch has continued to expand. Today, the president has substantial executive powers. For example, he can, without Congress, issue "Administrative Regulations," also called "Executive Orders," that have the power of law. If either or both houses of Congress are opposed to any of these regulations, they have to pass a law repealing the regulation that was authorized through the use of a power that the President has already been granted. And, of course, they would also need to override a presidential veto.

A consequence of these excessive executive powers is that the normal checks and balances that were put in place to stop bad laws, instead act to hobble Congress from preventing executive power abuse by the President's administrative departments, and in some cases independent agencies outside of even the President's control.

Most private-sector markets are fully capable of functioning without government interference. In these instances, the court system provides adequate protection to consumers who can claim actual damages from corporate abuse. However, there are business sectors where the free market doesn't function very efficiently on its own: healthcare, education, banking, public utilities, and infrastructure are some examples.

Post-Roosevelt progressivism is really about control. Politicians can wield an incredible amount of power and influence -- if voters give them control over the private sector. So, if a political party or movement can convince the country that capitalism is a corrupt, failed system, then it follows that voters will ask the government to intervene. Elected officials will therefore be free to enact a plethora of costly regulations that hamstring certain sectors, monopolize others, and ultimately raise consumer prices while simultaneously increasing our federal debt.

CHAPTER FOUR

Keynesianism: Stimulus, Deficits and Debt

Long run is a misleading guide to current affairs.
In the long run we are all dead.

John Maynard Keynes

The first economist to offer a complete and peer-accepted explanation for the Great Depression was the British economist, John Maynard Keynes *(1883-1946)*. His theory was simple: **Aggregate Demand** determines the overall level of economic activity, and that inadequate aggregate demand can lead to prolonged periods of high unemployment.

Keynes' reasoning went something like this: wealth dries up during an economic **Recession**; first consumers and then businesses stop spending money, causing a vicious circle where more consumers, who are now without jobs, have no money to purchase goods and services. Next, with diminishing consumer demand, industry has to slow production and lay off more workers who also have no money to buy goods and services, which drives economic activity even lower.

In his book the *General Theory of Employment Interest and Money* (1936), Keynes created a simplified model of how the major pieces of a market economy fit together. By utilizing his model, economists for decades have played guessing games as to the impact of certain government policies on growing **Gross Domestic Product** (GDP) and alleviating unemployment in a recession. He theorized that the solution to an economic recession (or depression) was for the federal government to intervene with a massive amount of spending, artificially spurring the demand for goods and services that the private sector would be unable to generate on its own. Keynes believed that the Great Depression could have been shortened by massive government stimulus spending. During this period, unemployment was extremely high while production and international trade tanked. In short, economic activity was grinding to a halt. A key element in Keynesian theory was that government inflationary spending should be used to give consumer demand a short-term boost. Once stimulated, the economy would respond by spurring production and increasing levels of employment. Theoretically, pulling the economy out of a recession.

Free Money?

William Phillips *(1914-1975)*, a New Zealand born economist, wrote a paper in 1958 titled *The Relation Between Unemployment and the Rate of Change of Money Wage Rates in the United Kingdom, 1861-1957.* As boring as the topic sounds, his theories regarding the relationship between inflation and unemployment have had a profound effect on modern economics. Expanding on Keynesian ideas, his research led him to develop the "Phillips Curve:" stated simply, the higher the rate of **Inflation**, the lower the unemployment in an economy.

The economic theories of Keynes and Phillips have become the backbone of modern economic policy -- Why? Because governments love the idea of free money! All U.S. Presidents have embraced these theories. The logic goes like this: full employment means significantly higher tax revenues than high levels of unemployment. Therefore, if the private sector is unable to provide a nation with continuous full employment, then Keynes and Phillips instruct governments to spend vast amounts of inflationary money to "prime-the-pump." This money is circulated through the economy and as a result of the **Multiplier Effect,** more and more money is generated until full employment is again achieved. The higher tax revenues pay for the new government spending and the budget is brought back into balance. To properly understand these concepts, I'll illustrate with a few simple examples.

The Multiplier Effect from Stimulus, a Micro Perspective

The Government sends me an $800.00 stimulus check; I purchase an $800.00 Dell computer at a local store; the store makes a deposit at the bank and uses part of the money to pay bills and make payroll; and then orders another computer from the manufacturer. The factory increases production by one unit and uses the money to pay bills, meet payroll, and purchase parts from vendors. Everyone and every company who benefits fractionally from this purchase will subsequently spend their portion of the $800.00, and those who receive the money will spend a portion of it and so on and so on.

The government's expenditure of $800 was a component of aggregate demand so it increased by $800; then, when I purchased the computer for $800, I increased consumer spending by $800, therefore, aggregate demand was increased by another $800.00. For simplicity, let's say that of the $800 purchase price, $400 is sent to Dell to replenish the store's inventory. Of that $400, let's assume that $100 stays in the U.S. and $300 goes to Mexico or Asia for the manufacture of one unit. The $100 adds to our domestic economic activity, the $300 does not. Let's just take a cursory glance at the first couple rounds of spending, federal government: $800, my computer purchase: $800, Dell's domestic portion: $100, the stores expenses, including profit: $400. To summarize: $800 + $800 + $100 + $400 = $2,100. It doesn't end there because the employees who receive a portion of the payroll will also spend their fraction of the total as will those who receive payment on bills and on and on and on. With each financial transaction from the original $800, domestic economic activity increases. Thus, the Multiplier effect. However, we must remember that so far, no new money was created. We only divvied up and circulated the original $800.

The Multiplier Effect from Stimulus, a Macro Perspective

For our next example, we have a hypothetical economy that is in a deep recession. The federal government responds by spending $1 trillion in economic stimulus. It does this by sending checks totaling $1 trillion dollars to every taxpayer as if it were a gift. Not all of this money, however, will increase economic activity in the United States. For example: 5.7% (our national savings rate) or $57 billion dollars will go into savings, leaving about $943 billion to spur economic activity.

Next, we need to take into account; U.S. taxpayers going on vacations to other countries, including cruises and U.S. taxpayers living abroad and/or purchasing properties abroad. We will look at these categories as a percentage of total U.S. consumer spending, which is reported at $11.7 trillion dollars. Therefore, once we have estimated our percentages, we can multiply them against our hypothetical $1 trillion-dollar stimulus. Americans spend about $158 billion on international travel and while there are no exact figures on Americans living abroad (and spending U.S. dollars) there are good estimates in the range of five to six million American "Expats" and overseas military personnel; so, if we extrapolate the average U.S. per capita income figure, reported at between $20,000 and $30,000, we can roughly determine the impact of these two categories at about 2.3% of total U.S. consumer spending. Therefore, we also need to deduct the 2.3% from our $1 trillion stimulus, which equals $23 billion; giving us a new sub-total of $920 billion dollars.

There is still one more category in which we need to account. Some of the money will be sent internationally to pay for imported products. As in the previous example, a portion of our computer purchase went to either Mexico or Asia. Likewise, perhaps an employee of the computer store, spent part of his or her paycheck on clothing that was manufactured in Southeast Asia. The portion of that purchase going overseas did not help stimulate the U.S. economy. Therefore, we need to further reduce the domestic economic impact of the stimulus by the total of imports which is about 17% of the

U.S. economy. 17% x $1 trillion = $170 billion. So, if we reduce our previous sub-total of $920 billion by $170 billion, then we are left with a grand total of $750 billion. In other words, the domestic economic impact of the government's stimulus package has been reduced by 25%.

Finally, as we saw in our last example; the money from my $800 stimulus check doesn't circulate forever through the economy; with each new round of spending the exchange of money becomes incrementally smaller. Therefore, economists estimate the limit of the multiplier effect to be about five times the original amount. $750 billion x 5 = $3.750 trillion. Okay, so $750 billion dollars is added to consumer spending and as it permeates throughout the economy, it's impact multiplies, but with each new financial transaction it will be diminished by 20%. However, as before, we still haven't created any new money, we simply divvied up and circulated the $1 trillion -- that if you remember, belonged to the taxpayers in the first place. In five rounds of spending we have gone from a total of $3.750 trillion to zero. I should also mention that a $1 trillion personal tax cut would accomplish exactly the same result as individual tax payers would have a commensurate amount of money in their wallets as a result of paying less in taxes.

For the purposes of our example it doesn't matter if the actual spending provided $1 trillion worth of value to our overall society or even if it provided any value at all, just so long as it circulated broadly throughout the economy. Thus, the circulation of currency became an end in itself. I don't mean to give the impression that currency floating around the country is as worthless as the wind blowing dust in circles. It clearly does have temporary value to the economy. Going back to our example, if I hadn't purchased the computer with my stimulus check, then theoretically it may have sat forever on the store's shelf. The store owner wouldn't have had the revenue to pay employees, pay bills, pay taxes or replenish his inventory with another computer. However, by temporary I mean that once this money has circulated throughout the economy, there is no real-world evidence to prove that it would significantly continue to spur spending and investment beyond the original $750 billion and truly bring a meaningful or permanent end to the recession. I should also remind you that $250 billion, of the original $1 trillion dollars spent by taxpayers, had no impact whatsoever on the U.S. economy.

But It's Good for the Politicians

Let's say for example that *without stimulus* the recession would have lasted for *three years*; and, that at the start of the recession, the federal government immediately spent $1 trillion to stimulate the sluggish economy. For the next three years unemployment goes down as the money circulates throughout the economy. Then, at the end of *three years* the economy magically recovers and the President brags that his policy brought an end to the recession. In the meantime, the trillion dollars is added to our long term national debt. Remember the wisdom of the old business axiom: "Never go into long-term debt to solve a short-term problem because you continue to pay for it long after the problem is solved." However, if the benefits of the stimulus coincide with the next election cycle, then the President's party will be rewarded with a victory at the polls! A pretty good political incentive. Wall Street investors also love stimulus because of a fixation on short term profits. And remember that as taxpayers this was our taxpayer money to begin with and the debt is ultimately our debt.

Inflation and Interest Rates

Deficit spending alone does not necessarily cause inflation. For example, deficit spending during a recession may not be inflationary because the private sector demand for currency goes down at the same time that currency demanded from the public sector goes up. Inflation kicks in when the private sector begins an economic expansion simultaneous with the government's new and insatiable demand for currency. Therefore, if the Federal Reserve Board (Fed) decides to keep interest rates low when the currency demanded by both private and public sectors is high, then the nation's money supply will sky-rocket above GDP -- resulting in inflation. Conversely, if the Fed restricts the nation's money supply with high interest rates, then inflation will be kept under control. This, in effect, is where the Fed uses interest rates as a tool to make sure the money supply grows at about the same rate as the overall economy. However, it isn't the private sector that causes the inflation, it is caused by deficit spending and the federal debt, in combination with low interest rates and other actions by the Federal Reserve Board that artificially expands the money supply.

It is the private sector and ultimately tax revenues that suffer when an economic boom is artificially curtailed by the Fed.

Creating Money

The United States has the ability to create and spend far more money than it collects in tax revenue by financing the deficit with Treasury Bonds. But how does the U.S. government use these to pay its bills once expenses exceed revenues?

- Method No. 1: The U.S. Treasury issues a United States Treasury Bond; the Bond is purchased by an individual, a corporation, a government or some other legal entity; then the money from the sale of the bond is deposited in the Treasury's account and used to pay expenses. The bond is backed by the full faith and credit of the United States. In other words, it is not backed by gold, silver, or any other collateral. It is an unsecured obligation of the United States government.

- Method No. 2: The U.S. government simply loans money to itself: The United States Treasury Department issues a Bond, which as previously mentioned is an instrument of debt. The Federal Reserve purchases the bond from the Treasury. Yes, one federal governmental agency issues the debt (The Treasury Department) and another quasi-federal government entity (The Federal Reserve System) purchases the debt. The Federal Reserve System pays for the Bond with a Federal Reserve Note, which is an obligation (debt) of the Federal Reserve System. Keep in mind that both Treasury Bonds and Federal Reserve Notes are ultimately both obligations of the United States of America. Sometimes the Federal Reserve System doesn't even bother to actually issue a Federal Reserve Note; through an accounting entry it simply credits the Treasury Department with the amount of money that would have been on the face of the Note. Yes, it is simply an accounting entry. Next, the Treasury Department deposits these Federal Reserve Notes into its checking account at a Federal Reserve Bank. It uses the money to write checks that can then pay expenses.

As you might expect, the process is a little more complicated than I have described: Federal Reserve Notes are backed by the assets of the twelve Federal Reserve Banks. Most of these assets, however, are United States Treasury Bonds, which have been purchased by commercial banks and deposited at the twelve Federal Reserve Banks. The commercial banks are required by law to take a certain percentage of their customer's deposits out of their bank vaults and use this money to purchase U.S. Treasury Bonds. If a commercial bank is short on cash, it can go to the Fed for a short-term loan. Also, if a bank is in financial difficulty, the Fed will step in to stabilize its finances or find a bank that will purchase its assets, if possible. Customer's deposits are insured up to $250,000 by the Federal Deposit Insurance Corporation (FDIC), which of course is another agency of the United States of America and is backed by its full faith and credit -- meaning United States taxpayers.

If you look at the above scenario in aggregate, the government uses the banking system to greatly expand its ability to spend and, in fact, create money, which can be done at will. The down side is that all this newly created money carries the risk of inflation, and the debt, regardless who holds it, eventually has to be repaid with interest.

In the end, because there are no hard assets, like gold or silver, to back up the debt, if there is ever a default by our federal government, the whole system will collapse like a house of cards!

Back to Keynes

If you remember, an economic recession is evidenced by extraordinarily weak aggregate demand. As we know, government spending is a component of aggregate demand. So, according to Keynes a massive infusion of government spending into the economy will kick-start consumer spending, and thanks to the multiplier effect will circulate throughout the economy, spurring production and increasing employment. This is intended to reduce government expenditures on unemployment insurance and welfare, and hopefully, more money will be paid in taxes increasing state and federal revenues.

But does it really work? It's pretty obvious that "Full Employment" will never be 0%. Economists can't even agree on its definition. According to a January 29, 2017 blog by the *Economist*, Janet Yellen *(1946-)*, a previous Federal Reserve Chair, believed that with an unemployment rate at 4.7% the U.S. was close to maximum employment. In other words, if the unemployment rate were to go much lower the Fed should raise interest rates to effectively "cool down" the economy. However, according to the same blog, only 69% of American adults have a job. And in many states, laid-off workers are only on the unemployment rolls for five months; afterwards, they are no longer counted in unemployment statistics -- whether or not they have found work.

Since 1948, the lowest official unemployment rate enjoyed by the U.S. economy was back in May of 1953 with a rate of 2.5%. The highest was 10.8% back in 1982, during Ronald Reagan's *(1911-2004)* first term in office and Paul Volcker's *(1927-)* first term as Federal Reserve Chairman.

With only a few exceptions, the U.S. has been operating a budget deficit every year since the 1930's. Meanwhile, our federal debt has gone from about $257 billion (about $2.34 trillion in today's dollars) in 1950 to $20 trillion today. So much for deficit spending paying for itself. In the meantime, recessions have come and gone in accordance with general business cycles, just as they have throughout history. In fact, as we discovered earlier in the chapter, there is no way to prove that government stimulus has had any significant impact on long-term national unemployment.

The first problem with Keynes is that stimulus spending has historically been project oriented. The federal dollars certainly help the companies (and their employees) contracted to repair roads and bridges, and build buildings. And, there is also a positive effect on the communities where the work is being done, however, the benefits are primarily localized and scattered unevenly around the country (The most powerful members of Congress typically make sure that their districts get the bulk of the money.) We should keep in mind, however, that if the projects were needed anyway, then it wasn't stimulus spending; it was simply the federal government freeing up funds that it needed to spend anyway. It is worthy of mention that in cases where these projects add more value to society than their cost, the money is well spent; however, the value is not in stimulus but in the intrinsic value of the projects.

The second problem is that the multiplier effect is limited. I previously gave the example of my imaginary computer purchase. Let's hypothetically multiply that by 50,000 purchases all made by taxpayers who received stimulus checks. All of the stores that benefited from this boondoggle increased their sales and profits, but only temporarily. So maybe for a few months their stores were a little busier than normal and maybe they added some temporary employees -- but once the stimulus money was gone, their businesses went back to previous levels. The effects going up the supply chain were also temporary. Factories receiving more orders may have temporarily increased production, added a third shift and hired some employees, but only after first reducing inventory levels. Smart companies would not have made major investment decisions in new factories, equipment or human resources -- based on a short-term increase in orders. In addition, their production facilities may be in Mexico or China, not the United States. In other words, the government stimulus did little more than create a temporary bubble in the economy. Because it was temporary, it simply confused the natural economy, making business decisions more difficult.

The third problem is inflation. We know that the holder of a treasury bond assumes a risk that the issuing nation will never repay its debt and the bond holder will be stuck holding a worthless piece of paper. But who is at risk with inflation? Holders of the inflationary currency; in our case U.S. dollars and dollar-based assets. Why? Because every year those dollars are worth less, and consequently the purchasing power of the dollar is less, meaning that products and services cost more, reducing our standard of living. Not everyone is lucky enough to have their earnings adjusted for inflation.

In the 1950's, the average house cost about $17,000, a gallon of gas cost 20 cents and you could purchase a full-size car for under $1,800. Overall, the purchasing power of a dollar in 1951 is equivalent to about $10 today. In other words, just in my lifetime, the dollar has lost 90% of its value!

The fourth problem is that inflation confuses the market. There is always a lag between the actual reduction in the currency's value and the market's ability to make proper price adjustments. With high inflation, companies have a very difficult time assessing true market demand, setting wages, making purchasing decisions, properly valuing inventory, and knowing what future interest rates will be charged by banks -- all of which makes accurate business planning difficult. And finally, remember that inflationary government spending was supposed to reduce unemployment; however, we learned in the 1970's that the strategy does not necessarily work. In fact, inflation actually worsens the unemployment problem. Because of high prices people spend less, which cause companies to lose sales, lower capital investment, and reduce employment levels.

The fifth problem is related to the idea that money is wealth. Money is simply the instrument or medium of exchange. True wealth, as explained by Adam Smith, is represented by the goods and services that money can purchase. Therefore, a nation is not wealthier because it prints more money. So, whether inflation occurs or not, the decision by governments to spend money, simply to stimulate the economy -- by filling a perceived gap in aggregate demand -- is inherently foolish. The problem is value. Every dime that the government spends should add more value to society than it costs the taxpayer, and every dime should be in accordance with good governance. As a base of comparison, let's look at a private-sector company. The goal should be to provide the customer with a product or service that is priced less than its value to the customer. This value could be intrinsic to the product; or the value could be derived from its convenience, or from providing the customer with outstanding service. But in any case, the value is not determined by the company but by the customer. Therefore, to maximize value to the customer and profit to the company, every employee must provide more value to his or her employer than they are paid in wages. Every business expense and every investment must return more value to the company than its cost. The same should be true with government spending. Every dime that the government spends should add more value to society than its cost to taxpayers.

The sixth problem is to blame insufficient aggregate demand as the source of unemployment. History has proven over and over that consumers have an unlimited desire for products and services. This demand is only constrained by purchasing power, which is a function of three factors: personal debt, savings and personal income. Personal debt is limited by the lendable value of your assets, like your home and automobile, and your ability to borrow unsecured funds based on your income and credit history. So, once the lendable equity in your home is used up and your credit cards are maxed out, you have hit a wall and your spending is limited to savings and personal income alone. Also, your net income (purchasing power) is reduced by the monthly payments on your debt.

Public sector jobs are necessary and desirable, but only to the extent that they provide more in value to society than their cost. In my opinion there should be a huge demand for valuable, tax supported jobs in the future, primarily in health care, education, energy and the rebuilding of our aging infrastructure.

Let's take another look at the multiplier effect, only this time we'll spend $1 trillion on infrastructure. We will still have the temporary benefit of stimulated employment, primarily in construction related fields. However, once the projects are finished there will still be long term benefits to society: A new bridge, for example will last for decades. The water supply in Flint, Michigan was recently worse than many third world countries and Flint is just the tip of the iceberg, as many cities around the country are in desperate need of new water and sewer lines. New and improved levees around the country would prevent much of the devastation caused by flooding. New high speed, high tech rail system would not only be safer but provide a much more efficient mode of transportation in and between major cities. Rush hour traffic in Los Angeles, Chicago and New York all show the gross inadequacy of our transportation systems. Also, our airports are old, overcrowded, and inefficient.

In addition, there is a tremendous need to transform our energy infrastructure away from coal and gas. And finally, there are huge unmet healthcare needs in this country that cannot be met under our current convoluted and overpriced health care system. In 2013, U.S. government spending on health care was $5,960 per capita (per person), which was the highest of any country in the world, including those with universal health care coverage. Yet even with Obamacare we still have 10% of the population, about 28 million people, not covered by health insurance!

Private Sector Jobs

The last and perhaps most significant example of the multiplier effect is related to business investment. Let's hypothetically say that a corporation decides to build a factory in your community, and the useful life of the building is forty years. The total cost to build and equip this plant is $50 million. The company hires 1000 total workers at an average salary of $40,000 per year. The total annual payroll is therefore $40 million. This includes management and supervision, engineering, Information Technology, maintenance, purchasing, production planning, and skilled, and unskilled workers. If we multiply this number by 75%, we get an initial economic benefit of $30 million. But because of the multiplier effect, the total economic benefit is five times $30 million or $150 million. This is triple the original investment of $50 million! And not one dime of taxpayer money was used. In fact, in addition to providing $150 million of annual economic bang, the company also pays federal state and local taxes that result from this one facility. The best part is that instead of providing only a temporary employment boost, this one will last 40 years. Finally, every time there is a purchase of the products produced by the factory then economic activity again multiplies. If we multiply this example by thousands of similar investments, the economy is truly in a boom. And with this boom comes an upward pressure on wages, raising the standard of living for millions of workers. As explained earlier, a true private sector economic expansion would increase domestic and international trade, encouraging huge new investments, which would lower unemployment rates and increase revenues to the federal government.

In spite of all evidence to the contrary, Keynesian-based theories are still taught as gospel on college campuses and are used as the basis for most government policies. It has become accepted in American politics that if we are in a recession, then the President or the political party in power is to blame. Economists, journalists, commentators, and even Hollywood celebrities demand that if unemployment rates are unacceptably high, then the government better fix things and fast! Decades of political promises, lies, and economic nonsense has seriously confused the American people to the point of utter desperation.

What they don't seem to realize is that recessions and expansions are a normal part of the business cycle, and that these business cycles are industry specific. For example, in the late 1970's the energy and technology sectors as well as associated geographical regions like southern Texas and Silicon Valley were in an expansion. During the same period, however, Automotive was in a recession, which affected Michigan and other heavily industrialized states. In fact, so many workers were leaving Michigan for boom cities like Houston that a popular bumper sticker stated: "Will the last person leaving Michigan please turn off the lights?"

When calculating GDP, government statisticians combine all business sectors and geographic regions; and then totals them together. This means that at any given time the nation may officially be in a recession but specific industries (and specific regions of the country) may be experiencing an expansion, or vice versa. So even if you implemented a complicated policy mechanism to kick-start an artificial influx of industry-specific demand using taxpayer money, all that would be accomplished is a short-term reduction in the industry's inventory levels; a short-term boost in industry-related employment and profits; a delay in the industry-related recession; and confusion in the true marketplace for the industry's products. In actual practice, Congress and the President have used economic stimulus as nothing more than a political tool to reward supporters and hope for a temporarily improvement in the unemployment rate until the next election. In any case, as a result of decades of political interference the economy is weaker and more dysfunctional; and we the people are stuck with the debt.

In retrospect, **Stagflation** in the 1970's; the demise of the Savings and Loans in the 1980's, and the Banking/Real Estate meltdown of 2008-2011 were all symptoms of our federal debt crisis which will continue to plague us, and in fact worsen, until we can get a grip on both our federal budget and debt.

Too Much Debt

Can you imagine what wonderful projects could be undertaken if the United States today had $20 trillion dollars to spend for the betterment of society? This denominational figure represents our federal debt; every dime of which was over and above government revenues! Most depressing is not the enormity of the debt, but that most of the money spent was either allocated to or influenced by special-interests; meaning that these politically connected groups benefited at the expense of our country at large. Today, we still have huge unmet needs in this country, and $20 trillion dollars of debt!

The relationship between our federal revenue and public debt can be compared to a family with an annual income of $40,000 taking out a mortgage for $256,000. With no other debt, the maximum amount that a bank might qualify this family for a loan is under $200,000. Financially speaking, you might say they are pretty stretched and so is our federal government; but that's not the end of the story. What I did not mention is that the unfunded liabilities of the United States Government are approximately $100 trillion and growing! This is mostly for federal retirement, Social Security and Medicare, which if combined with our public debt is over 40 times the federal government's gross income. These programs are called "Entitlements" or "Transfer Payments", because as tax revenues are received by the federal government they are simply transferred to the recipients of these programs. In fact, a large share of every dollar that the federal government receives in revenue goes directly to one of these many entitlement programs. Most of the remaining budget is added to the deficit and included in our federal debt.

Going back to our family earning $40,000 per year and multiplying it by 40, we have a comparable family debt of $1,600,000. Wow! The obvious question is: how can a family with a total annual income of $40,000 ever pay back $1.6 million? Or put another way: how can a government with total annual revenues of $3.5 trillion ever pay back $120 trillion? And if that's not bad enough according to the Congressional Budget Office there is no end in sight to our annual budget deficits, which means that the federal debt will also continue to grow, as will our unfunded liabilities. Just look at the growth trajectory of our federal debt over the past 25 years.

- 1992   Federal Debt: $4 trillion
- 2002   Federal Debt: $6.2 trillion
- 2012   Federal Debt: $16 trillion
- 2018   Federal Debt $20 trillion

I want to emphasize that every dime the government spends has to eventually be paid for in taxes, including the national debt.

When President Obama sent all taxpayers a 2009 stimulus check, the $600.00 that I received (along with the money received by every other taxpayer) will eventually have to be paid back to the government, plus interest: so, it wasn't really a gift, it was more like a loan that will affect future taxpayers. In the long run, stimulus plans, boondoggle projects, make-work programs and all forms of frivolous government spending are bad for the economy and bad for the wealth of the nation.

Zero Sum Gain

A common argument used to oppose the expansion of government programs is that they represent a *Zero-sum gain* (or game) to society. Some zero-sum examples from our federal government include:

- Loan guarantees: $535 million went to the bankrupt Solyndra Corporation.
- Crop subsidies: The 2014 farm bill budgeted subsidies to be $90 billion over ten years.
- Most foreign aid projects: the Obama Administration spent $20 million to help Indonesian students obtain masters degrees.
- Federal grants: $615,000 to digitalize memorabilia from the drug-obsessed, counterculture band, Grateful Dead; and $103,000 to find out if sunfish that drink tequila are more aggressive than sunfish that drink gin.
- Military cost overruns: The F-35 Joint Strike Fighter Jet is $163 billion over-budget.
- Every omnibus spending bill is burdened with billions of dollars in congressional pork barrel spending.

These are all examples of direct costs to United States taxpayers that benefit politically-connected individuals, organizations, corporations, and nations, which result in a net gain to our economy and society of zero.

To further illustrate the point: if you hand over a $100 bill to a thief at gunpoint, then you are $100 poorer and the thief is $100 richer, the net gain in wealth is zero. On the other hand, if you purchase $100 worth of groceries at the supermarket, then in aggregate the items in your shopping cart are more valuable to you than the $100 that you give to the cashier. The economy and society gain from the excess value over cost because, not only did you gain from the transaction, but so did the growers, the manufacturers, the distributors, and the retail store.

Deficit Spending Is Cumulative

Remember that deficit spending is cumulative and that, with only minor exceptions, since the 1930's, the federal government has never actually paid off any of its loans. When a federal bond comes due, the treasury writes a check to the bond holder with money that it borrowed from the sale of a new bond. Therefore, money borrowed by FDR during the new deal and World War II are still buried in our $20 trillion debt.

Finally, as I stated earlier, if there was no federal debt, then interest rates could be kept stable and predictable. At the same time, the Federal Reserve could provide ample increases in the money supply to fuel a true economic expansion. This would consequently keep unemployment low, tax rates low and more tax revenues to pay for our necessary government services.

The federal government wants us to pretend that in 2017 it was acceptable to spend $4 trillion, even though revenues were only $3.3 trillion (And the proposed 2018 budget predicts a deficit of $1 trillion). We are supposed to forget that the $700 billion difference is piling-on to our national debt. In other words, Congress will spend whatever it wants and leave the $700 billion for our children, grandchildren, or future international bail-out funds to worry about. Oh wait -- there won't be enough wealth in the world to bail out the

United States because the rest of the world will likely be in worse shape than us.

Keynes Dream

In 1930, Keynes wrote an essay titled: *Economic Possibilities for our Grandchildren*. Like Adam Smith and Karl Marx before him he was concerned with technological advances and the painful readjustments that would result from the replacement of labor with improvements in technology. Keynes, however, had an optimistic outlook for the future, believing that by the year 2030 standards of living would be vastly greater than in his time. He predicted that the standard workweek would shrink to only 15 hours per week and that we would, through improved technology, still be able to produce enough to live happy and fulfilled lives.

Today, our standard of living has definitely improved since 1930; however, the average workweek is not yet what he predicted. Only 8% of fulltime employees work less than 40 hours, 42% work 40 hours and 50% work over 40 hours per week. Corporate America implemented a plan different from what Keynes predicted. Rather than spreading productivity improvements over all of its existing employees and reducing their work hours accordingly, it instead reduced its work force (through layoffs and firings) to fit 40 hours for non-exempt employees (not exempt from the labor law requiring employers to pay overtime), and 40-plus hours for exempt employees -- the company can force these employees to work unlimited hours without paying anything over their standard salaries. Thus, companies have taken all of the productivity gains as profit, which is what Marx would have predicted. Of course, it was the companies who invested in the technology, so shouldn't their owners reap the benefits, not their employees? Hmmm, debatable.

CHAPTER FIVE

Greenspanianism: Monetary Stimulus

*I don't know where the stock market is going, but I will say
this, that if it continues higher, this will do more to stimulate
the economy than anything we've been talking about
today or anything anybody else was talking about.*
Alan Greenspan (1926-), former Chairman, Federal Reserve

In the last chapter, we looked primarily at fiscal stimulus. The difference between fiscal and monetary stimulus is somewhat nuanced, but important. Fiscal stimulus starts with Congress and the President deciding to spend taxpayer money over and above normal levels with the intent of stimulating the economy. The Federal Reserve has no option, but to allow the money supply to grow with the new demand created by government spending. The treasury will then print money well beyond the nation's GDP. The resulting inflation will supposedly kick-start the multiplier effect and end the economic downturn. Over time, however, long-term inflation simply becomes an expected and normal part of economic life; market adjustments are made; and consequently, even short term stimulus is ineffective at reducing unemployment. A similar phenomenon occurs with protracted periods of artificially low interest rates.

Monetary stimulus is a stimulus plan independent of fiscal policy and driven by the Federal Reserve. As was discussed earlier, an artificial, short term lowering of interest rates will cause a rise in the money supply which temporarily increases economic activity. Unlike fiscal stimulus with its consumer price inflation, the economy experiences "Asset Inflation." This means that the benefits of monetary stimulus are disproportionally tilted to industries sensitive to interest rates, like banking, finance, the stock market and real estate; meaning, that a disproportionate percentage of the nation's GDP goes to these industries.

Since the Federal Reserve Board is comprised of bankers, and members of the Federal Reserve System are banks, and between 2002 and 2008 bank assets were heavily tilted toward the stock market and real estate, its pretty easy to see why encouraging asset inflation was the Fed's primary goal. On the other hand, a booming increase in the general economy would incite wage and price inflation -- which would be curtailed by the Fed.

The stock market is affected by low interest rates because low interest rates discourage savers, who look for a better return in the equity markets. The new influx of money from savings accounts and bonds now rushes to the stock market. Therefore, when you increase demand without a corresponding increase in supply, the price goes up. As stock prices rise, a bull market ensues, causing the market version of a feeding frenzy. When the markets stabilize, they settle at elevated prices.

There are three downsides to this policy. First, over time low interest rates become an expected and normal part of economic life, nulling the benefits of stimulus. Second, it creates a bubble in the affected industries that will collapse when interest rates are eventually returned to natural levels, which must eventually happen. Or, the bubble will burst when the markets are stretched to the breaking point, usually coupled with the start of a recession. Third, low interest rates encourage debt and discourage saving. Debt-driven growth creates an exaggerated economic collapse. This is because the leverage used to spur the economy (magnifying corporate profits; and gains in real estate and stocks) will equally exacerbate the recession.

Bretton Woods Agreement

After World War II, the *Bretton Woods System* was established. Under this international agreement, the United States dollar was to be pegged to the price of gold, and the world's currencies would then be pegged to the dollar. This system, however, conflicted with a new goal of the Federal Reserve, which was to couple monetary and fiscal policy to stimulate the economy, thus reducing unemployment [1]. This, as we discussed earlier, meant an increase in inflation.

During the 1950's and 1960's inflation was low and the economy was booming with low unemployment rates, but just below the surface there was a huge boom in public spending. The Vietnam War was in full swing and President Lyndon Johnson *(1908-1973)* declared war on poverty in America, calling his new policy "The Great Society." This created a huge demand for currency at the same time that the private sector, still in its boom, also demanded increases in the money supply, setting the stage for inflation and for a recession in the 1970's. Being loyal Keynesians, this meant keeping interest rates low and hoping that a policy of continued inflation would end the recession. To that end, Richard Nixon *(1913-1994)* abandoned the Bretton Woods System in 1971; and suspended the backing of our currency with gold.

The Monetarists

The first hint that the Keynes/Phillips model was flawed came during this period in the 1970's. Our economy experienced a prolonged period of both high unemployment and high inflation, called "stagflation." Peaking in 1981, the annual inflation rate soared to 13.5%. In just one decade, the dollar had lost half its value! Economists everywhere were in a panic trying to explain this new phenomenon. If you remember, high inflationary spending was supposed to kick start the multiplier-effect, dramatically increasing aggregate demand and spurring production to higher and higher levels, which would lower the unemployment rate.

Along came Milton Friedman *(1912-2006)* from the Chicago School of Economics, father of the Monetarist movement. He was the first to criticize the Phillips Curve, and back in the 1960's correctly predicted the stagflation that occurred a decade later. Friedman, who was a fiscal conservative, believed that inflation was not a stable strategy for reducing unemployment. Instead, he favored a policy of monetary neutrality. The Central Bank's role would be to match the money supply with the total dollar value of goods and services actually produced in the economy (GDP).

As mentioned earlier, Keynes and Phillips believed that there was a direct correlation between unemployment and inflation. High unemployment indicated a slack in the economy which could cause disinflation and even deflation (where prices trend downward). Therefore, by injecting inflationary spending into the economy, that slack would be removed and employment would rise. Simply, they believed it impossible for high inflation and high unemployment to coexist. Friedman correctly pointed out that prolonged periods of inflation would become expected and structurally part of the market economy. Thus, as mentioned before, the tool of inflationary stimulus during prolonged periods of inflation would have no impact on reducing unemployment. Economists have since revised their Keynesian models to reflect this newly discovered reality.

The first real test for Monetarism came in the early 1980's with Paul Volcker, the first monetarist Federal Reserve Chairman. When he took office our nation's money supply was growing at a much faster rate than GDP due to inflationary government spending. He initially tried, unsuccessfully, to convince Congress to show fiscal restraint. When that didn't work, he turned U.S. Monetary Policy upside down.

It had previously been the long-term practice of the Federal Reserve Board to maintain the Federal Funds Rate (the rate to which member banks are able to borrow money from the Federal Reserve Bank) within a narrow range consistent with monetary growth objectives set by the Fed. This gave the nation's money supply ample room to swing with the natural demand for currency. Because inflation was such a huge national problem, Volcker decided to restrict the money supply, not through the control of interest rates, but by managing the volume of bank reserves in the system. This new policy allowed interest rates to fluctuate with the market. As we previously discussed, according to the simple law of supply and demand when you decrease the supply of a commodity (in this case money) without a corresponding decrease in demand, then the price (in this case interest rates) will go up.

Suddenly, interest rates exploded! Banks were paying 14 to 15% on six-month certificates of deposit. The Federal Funds Rate jumped to 20%. The interest rate that banks were offering to their best business loan customers the "Prime Rate" shot up to a high of 21.5%. And this was at a time when in most parts of the country, under state *Usury Laws*, the maximum legal interest rate that banks could charge on credit card debt was 18%.

Demise of the Savings & Loan Industry

Let's compare the economy to a living organism. If you restrict the flow of blood to a certain part of the body, you have what is known as a stroke. A stroke can cause partial paralysis: brain damage, speech impairment, etcetera. Any part of the body that is deprived of blood will soon cease to function. The same is true with money.

The *Savings and Loan industry* (also known as *Thrifts* or *Building and Loans*) began back in 1816 and flourished through the 19th and most of the 20th centuries. By law, they were only allowed to offer savings accounts, including certificates of deposit, and could only make mortgage loans against single-family homes. During the 1970's these institutions paid passbook savers an interest rate of about 5%. The depositor's money was then loaned out at 7% or 8%, earning the Savings & Loan an interest spread of about 2% or 3%. Stable interest rates were necessary for the economic viability of the Savings and Loan industry and to a lesser extent, commercial banks. Because of Paul Volcker's new policy, the cost of funds skyrocketed and with their primary assets fixed at an average yield of around 7%, the entire industry was having a massive stroke!

The business model used by banks and S&L's relied on stable interest rates especially for their long-term mortgage assets. When it became clear that this was no longer true, the government needed to step in and save the entire financial services sector. Reagan's solution was to dramatically deregulate the entire banking and Savings & Loan industries. So, with congressional support a number of laws were passed that removed depression-era safeguards. The intent was to give more freedom to the financial services sector, hoping that new avenues of lending and investments would strengthen these sick institutions. They were also now allowed to compete and/ or merge with major stock brokerage firms. In addition, reserve requirements for the S&L's were greatly reduced, allowing thinly capitalized firms to loan many times their net worth, often on risky **Loan Participations**. Suddenly a new wave of speculative lending and investments flooded both industries at the same time that the economy was headed toward a recession. The result was disastrous!

Dozens of banks failed and hundreds more were in serious trouble. The largest was Continental Illinois National Bank with assets of $45 billion, partly as a result of holding tens of millions of dollars in worthless loan participations from the infamous Penn Square Bank. In 1984 Congress authorized a $4.5 billion bailout, fearing a chain reaction of more bank failures. Several major banks tied to Continental breathed a sigh of relief.

By the late 1980's Congress authorized The Resolution Trust Corporation, which was charged with managing and liquidating the assets of hundreds of failed Savings and Loans. Between 1989 and mid-1995, the Resolution Trust Corporation closed or otherwise resolved 747 thrifts with total assets of $394 billion.

On a more positive note, Volcker's policies worked. By the mid-1980's inflation had been wrung out of the system, and the recession ended just in time for Reagan to win a second term. Subsequent Federal Reserve Chairmen have continued as inflation watchdogs, but that hasn't stopped them from using their power over interest rates and the money supply to affect, or at least attempt to affect, specific markets. The first example came in 1987, when in response to a 508-point drop in the Dow Jones Industrial Average (DJIA), Alan Greenspan lowered interest rates. He believed that by expanding the money supply, more money would flow back into the stock market, and that industries like banking and real estate (sensitive to changes in interest rates) would boom. The market did recover and continued to expand even when the Fed raised interest rates in the mid-90's. In fact, from 1995 to 2000 the DJIA was growing at a clip of 15% per year. The NASDAQ index was doing even better, largely driven by technology stocks.

Then the bubble burst! First, in 1998, the enormous hedge fund Long Term Capital Management (LTCM) collapsed. Of the $1 trillion held in derivatives, $125 billion was borrowed from major New York banks. In the end, the Fed arranged for a $3.5 billion-dollar bailout, rescuing Lehman Brothers and other banks. This led Wall Street to believe that the federal government would continue to be a safety net for the big banks, encouraging highly leveraged and risky investments. The LTCM collapse preceded another big stock market crash. Between 2000 and 2002, the total market value of New York Stock Exchange (NYSE) and NASDAQ companies combined went from $18.3 trillion to $9 trillion. The Fed responded again by lowering interest rates. Only this time, Greenspan kept them artificially low, even as the economy heated up; which it continued to do until the "Great Recession" hit in 2008.

Between 2003 and 2008 the economy seemed to be doing just fine. Stock prices, real estate values and GDP were all rising and unemployment rates were trending down. But, just below the surface there were serious dysfunctions. First, job growth in the private sector was non-existent. Second, wealth in the United States was moving from a manufacturing-based economy to financial services. Even big traditional manufacturers Like General Electric and General Motors had set up huge finance divisions; and not just to finance commercial equipment and automobiles, but to get in on the now lucrative mortgage business. Third, low interest rates were causing a refinance boom. People were taking out second, even third mortgages, and spending the money. This created a debt-fueled expansion:

According to US Federal Reserve estimates, in 2005 homeowners extracted $750 billion of equity from their homes, up from $106 billion in 1996; spending two thirds of it on personal consumption, home improvements, and credit card debt [1].

Fourth, deregulation of the banking industry, easy money, and rising real estate prices (rising collateral values provided a cushion to banks in the case of mortgage defaults), set the stage for a booming derivatives market to insure the mortgage-backed bonds. Further, there evolved a view among bankers that the federal government would bail them out of any difficulties. These were the major factors that encouraged banks to over-leverage themselves and take on increasing risky investments, which in turn led to the Great Recession.

When the Great Recession ended, there was such weak demand for currency that the Fed implemented a program called "Quantitative Easing," which was a policy of purchasing massive amounts of mostly long-term government bonds, artificially lowering mortgage rates. They also lowered the Fed Funds rate to zero, buoying the money supply. The goal was to once again, stimulate the sick banking and real estate industries. Remember Albert Einstein's famous quote: "The definition of insanity is doing the same thing over and over again but expecting different results."

Let's step back for a minute. From 1990 to 2008, nearly all job growth came from service based businesses and government. Health care was the biggest jobs creator, followed by government (and education accounted for nearly 70% of government jobs).

Economist Michael Mandel has shown that, between February of 2001 and February 2011 employment in the U.S. economy in health care, education and government increased by 16%. This was not simply a function of a growing population and economy. During the same period, employment outside of those sectors decreased by 8% [2].

While there is plenty of blame to go around, actions taken by the Federal Reserve contributed not only to the mortgage crises but also to changes in the economy that lowered employment in the private sector, particularly manufacturing.

A Difficult Balancing Act

The Federal Reserve has no control over government spending and very little control over health care spending (partly due to Medicaid and Medicare, and partly due to the power of the various health lobbies). It, does however, have significant control over the rest of the private sector. In other words, government and health care spending will continue to rise regardless of interest rates. The private sector will not. Therefore, the balancing act is to allow enough money into circulation to keep the economy from falling into recession; but fearing inflation, they will not allow enough money to fuel what we all really want -- a true economic expansion.

As you remember, it was the long-term policy of the United States to maintain stable interest rates. The money supply was allowed to fluctuate with market demand. This policy worked fine until inflationary government spending (at the time it was the result of the Vietnam War and President Johnson's Great Society programs) increased the money supply well beyond the true growth of the economy (GDP). The dollars were consequently worth less and therefore prices were driven up. Federal Reserve under Chairman Volcker stopped this cycle by dramatically allowing interest rates to rise. And since that time the Fed has maintained a low inflation policy for the past thirty years and for the past thirty years the private sector economy has sputtered along while the growth in health care and federal government spending has skyrocketed. So, until the federal government is brought under control we will never see a true private sector boom because the Fed, fearing that an increased upward pressure on wages and prices (caused by an increased demand for products, services and labor) will create high private-sector demand for currency at the same time the public-sector demand for currency is already high. Therefore, fearing inflation, the Fed will respond, as it did under Volker, by raising interest rates to artificially high levels. This will reduce the money supply, squashing the boom. Meanwhile, the Fed is repeating the asset inflation that led to the crash in 2008. Since 2013, the 4% difference between the growth in our money supply (M2) and growth in goods and services (GDP) would normally be inflationary – but the extra currency has only modestly driven-up consumer prices; the remainder has inflated stocks and real estate.

Price Bubbles

Let's take a minute to look at "Price Bubbles," also known as a "Speculative," or "Economic Bubbles." In any market, you have both the supply for a product or commodity and a demand for it. Price is the tool that brings these two forces into equilibrium. However, sometimes demand can be temporary or artificially induced. Let's say for example that a military base moves into a metropolitan area, bringing with it a large number of potential home buyers. Home prices explode and there is a sudden surge in new home and apartment building construction. The entire local economy benefits, with new businesses, such as restaurants, hotels, etcetera. Finally, the local real estate market reaches equilibrium and home prices stabilize at a much higher level than before the boom. Keep in mind that the value of each house is still approximately the same as it was before; however, the value of the land (Location, Location, Location.) has risen because of its proximity to the base. Then, fast-forwarding 20 years into the future, the Department of Defense decides to close the base. The resulting real estate crash is also the bursting of the price bubble. The Department of Defense artificially inflated the housing market when it built the base, creating the bubble. Then, when the base pulled out of the community, it burst the bubble sending real estate prices tumbling.

The stock market is currently experiencing an expanding price bubble based on the same principal. The 2017 inflation rate

(Consumer Price Index) was 2.1%. On the other hand, a one-year bank Certificate of Deposit was paying a rate of 2%. This means that adjusted for inflation, savers were earning a negative rate of interest. On the other hand, in March of 2009 the Dow Jones Industrial Average was about 6,600. Six years later the DJIA was approximately 18,000. Today the Dow is hovering around 25,000, representing a 379% gain! And this is just the average of the 30 blue chip companies on which the index is comprised. The two potential events that could burst the bubble would be: first, a resurgence of inflation that would force the Federal Reserve to significantly raise interest rates; or second, a recession, which would weaken corporate profits, causing out-of-whack Price-Earnings ratios, initiating a huge stock market selloff.

United States Department of the Federal Reserve?

I suppose we should be appreciative that the Federal Reserve System is not a department under the Executive Branch, because if they were, we would likely be faced with $20 trillion in debt and a 12% inflation rate! As good Keynesians, the executive and legislative branches of government have historically preferred unlimited increases in the debt limit and unlimited increases in the money supply in order to keep unemployment low, and to pay for an endless number of new government programs.

CHAPTER SIX

Bankism: The Domino Effect

*Some things never change - there will be another crisis,
and its impact will be felt by the financial markets.*
Jamie Dimon (1956-), Chairman, JP Morgan Chase

2008: The Banking Crises

The business model that commercial banks employed from the Great Depression to the Reagan Era ended in the 1980's. The financial services sector had long hated the *Glass-Steagall Act* which placed strict limits on a bank's ability to expand interstate or participate in the securities industry, not to mention the many restrictions placed on banking by the various state governments. As mentioned before, heavy lobbying received sympathetic ears from both the President and Congress, resulting in the complete dismantling of depression-era safeguards, and the continuation of monetary stimulus.

The products that affected the "Great Recession" were tied to mortgages in the following way: Let's say that John Doe buys a house. He then goes to his local bank and takes out a mortgage. His bank sells (assigns) the mortgage to another bank which acts as servicer of the loan. The mortgage is then sold (assigned) to the investment banking division of another bank who consolidates his mortgage with hundreds of other mortgages. All of these mortgages will be securitized into a mortgage-backed bond. The bond will then be turned over to stockbrokers who sell them as securities. Meanwhile, the Investment banking group has created a new company called a "Special Purpose Vehicle" (SPV). To expand on this example, the investment banking group sells the bond, along with the underlying mortgages, including the income stream from mortgage payments made by the mortgage borrowers, packaged with hundreds of other bonds, to the SPV. The SPV then creates and issues a funded (collateralized) credit instrument (which is a form of mortgage-backed bond), called a "Collateralized Debt Obligation" or (CDO). Each CDO is sliced into "tranches." These catch the cash flow of the interest and principal payments based on the seniority of the tranche.

The capital structure of a tranche fell in different investment classes from: Equity Class to Unrated Subordinated, to BB to BBB to AA to AAA to AAA Plus to Super Senior AAA. These classes were established by credit reporting agencies. If the underlying mortgages defaulted, the lowest or Equity Class would suffer the first losses, then the next lowest all the way up to Super Senior AAA tranches. The lower rated tranches received a higher interest rate based on the higher risk taken by the investor. Therefore, all the combined mortgages that had been consolidated into a bond, actually transferred to the investors, who owned pieces of the CDO. These instruments were sold to investors, including financial institutions all around the world. As new mortgages were made, the process was repeated over and over.

When the banking industry introduced a large number of bad or "toxic" mortgages into this process, you can see how these toxins were distributed worldwide, eventually collapsing the entire system, which, as we will see later, required several governments -- primarily the United States -- to bail them out.

Banks were not the only mortgage loan originators. A whole new industry evolved during the 2002-2008 real estate boom. In fact, the country's largest mortgage lender was Countrywide Financial, who by 2008 was near bankruptcy when Bank of America swooped in and bought the struggling mortgage company. There were thousands of less scrupulous firms and mortgage brokers who would make loans, pretty much to anyone who had a breath. No Income No Job (NINJA Loans)? That was okay. Bad credit? That was okay too. You needed more money than the lendable value of your house? No problem, they had real estate appraisers who would submit a falsified report, which exaggerated it's value.

Looking at all this strictly from an investment perspective, these sub-prime, nonconforming mortgages (meaning that they did not conform to the underwriting requirements of "Freddie Mac" or "Fannie Mae") carried a higher interest rate which was attractive to investors. And they held rising collateral values that, under normal circumstance, would protect investors from foreclosure losses. In fact, if you look at a United States chart of real estate values from 1900 to 2008, you will see an almost continuous unbroken rise in real estate values that had been accelerating since the early 1990's. Therefore, investors expected only a minimal risk of loss, even by investing in the lowest equity class.

The practice was easily rationalized by mortgage lenders. After all, everyone wants to buy a bigger, better house in a nicer neighborhood. And no one put a gun to the heads of homebuyers and forced them into contracts that they could not afford. And, the lenders were only giving these borrowers what they wanted.

The following is a loose analogy: I worked with a couple of bank branch managers back in the mid-seventies. They were given adequate lending authority and profit responsibilities over their branches. Naturally, there was a constant push to grow the bank's business; so, these two managers started competing with each other to see who could make the most car loans. They both decided to throw generally accepted credit standards out the window and make car loans to anyone of legal age that walked in the door. One of the managers would lecture the loan applicants that went something like this: "Now, you normally wouldn't qualify for a loan, but I can see that you are a good person and need this car, so I am going to take a risk and make you the loan." Then he would ramble on about the importance of a good credit rating and would emphasize the great opportunity he was giving them to turn around their credit ratings;

and finally, the banker would obtain a promise that all payments would be made on time. He even took the time to cross-sell other bank services. The strategy worked great -- at first. Word of mouth spread and both bankers had customers lining-up for loans. Upper management gave them both accolades and never questioned their methods. In, fact they were so successful that the younger, more aggressive banker was promoted from Branch Manager to Assistant Vice President. Then the delinquencies started piling up, which led to repossessions and losses to the bank. The older manager was asked to retire and the younger manager was fired. And all the high-risk bank customers that temporarily had cars -- but didn't make their payments – lost them to the bank.

Now, if the managers had been humanitarians and were risking their own capital then I would applaud their efforts to help their fellow citizens in need; however, it wasn't their money to risk, it was the bank's capital. And if this practice had been widespread, it wouldn't have just been the bank's capital at risk, but also the depositor's savings, which was insured by the federal government, so ultimately it would be the taxpayer's money at risk.

To summarize the mortgage crises: Shady lenders accumulated a portfolio of worthless loans, which were transferred to a special purpose company (SPV). Stock brokers would sell securities to investors, who incorrectly believed that the underlying mortgages were good loans, letting the original lenders completely off the hook. This may surprise you, but the above described process would have been a relatively minor historical event if not for the widespread misuse of derivatives.

Derivatives Defined

Any discussion of the Great Recession would not be complete without the topic of "derivatives." A derivative is a financial instrument that derives its value from an underlying asset. Let's take a simple example: A farmer agrees to sell one ton of barley to a brewery for $150. This creates a simple contract (offer, acceptance, and consideration).

For the next example, we simply introduce the element of time: the farmer anticipates having one ton of barley in 90 days, but the price of barley fluctuates every day. Let's assume that the farmer is happy with today's price and would rather not risk a lower price in 90 days. Fortunately for the farmer, a commodities trader comes along and offers a "Futures Contract," which guarantees him $150 for one ton of barley, 90 days in the future. Therefore, the trader has assumed his risk, sort of like an insurance policy against the potential of a price drop. If the price of barley goes up to $160, the trader makes a profit of $10. If it goes down to $140, then he suffers a $10 loss. The futures contract is an example of a derivative, because its value is derived from the fluctuating price of its underlying asset, in this case, barley.

You can see that investors in the various derivatives markets are speculators. To be successful, they must become experts in understanding the fundamental and/or technical aspects of the markets in which they speculate. There are two differences between these speculators and gamblers: first, the speculators, in most cases, add stability to the markets in which they participate (however, we will see that in 2008, a certain breed of derivatives contributed greatly to the meltdown.) Second, through research, speculators are able minimize their risk, whereas gamblers are at the mercy of "Lady Luck."

Derivatives -- Bankers Gone Wild

Back to Collateralized Debt Obligations (CDO's): for our next example the mortgage loan originator sells the debt to the Special Purpose Vehicle (SPV), the SPV subsequently forms a "Credit Default Swap" (CDS), which is a synthetic Collateralized Debt Obligation. Synthetic CDO's are derivatives. In the case of CDS's, the mortgage originators would keep the debt, but purchased protection on it, sort of like an insurance policy and similarly paid a premium to the CDS that was relative to the perceived risk. The lender would be paid par (his original investment) in case of any mortgage defaults in his portfolio. The losses instead would fall on the investors distributed through the capital structure of the tranche (Equity Class through AAA Plus). Remember, however, that the debt did not transfer, only the risk. Therefore, the bank had the ability to write multiple securitizations on the same portfolio. This is because the bank didn't have to actually transfer anything. Keep in mind that no due diligence was performed on any of these instruments, because the rating agencies assumed them to be extremely low risk [3].

Because you could put one synthetic CDO on top of another synthetic CDO, on top of another synthetic CDO (CDO's squared and even CDO's cubed), you put more distance between the investor and the risk -- therefore they seemed safer than products without derivatives. However, as it turned out, there was simply a straight line between the toxic loans and the investors. Eventually you had trillions of dollars of risk spread by the financial system around the globe. It was inevitable that this entire "Ponzi" type scheme would eventually collapse!

The Government Bailouts

- AIG $85 billion
- Morgan Stanley $107 billion
- Citigroup $99 billion
- Bank of America $91 billion
- Goldman Sachs $69 billion
- JP Morgan Chase $68 billion
- Royal Bank of Scotland $84 billion
- Deutsche Bank $66 billion
- Foreign Central Banks $583 billion
- Fannie Mae/Freddie Mac $169 billion
- Mortgage Backed Securities $1.2 trillion

In the end, the U.S. taxpayers paid -- through the Federal Reserve -- bailouts totaling $3.95 trillion. Additionally, between 2007 and 2009 over $13 trillion in emergency lending went to a handful of large financial institutions. It should be noted that the U.S. banking industry has since recovered and much of the bailout money, including regulatory fines, has been reimbursed to the federal government.

In the aftermath of the crisis, the market for mortgage-backed securities completely dried up, and Freddie Mac and Fannie Mae, which were already quasi-government entities, were taken over by the federal government, including their $1.3 trillion dollars of mortgage debt. This resulted in 98% of all mortgages in the country being held by the federal government, essentially nationalizing the mortgage industry.

Banking and the Federal Reserve

Banks are required by law to maintain with the Federal Reserve System a percentage of their total deposits in United States Government Bonds. For example, if you deposit $100 with your local bank, and the bank has a reserve requirement of 10%, then $10 of your deposit will be used by your bank to purchase these bonds. The bank earns interest from the bonds, which are held on deposit at one of the twelve Federal Reserve Banks.

As you recall, taxpayers, through the FDIC are on the hook for all customer deposits up to $250,000 per individual -- just in case the bank goes bust! Therefore, there are two main reasons for the reserve requirement: The Federal Reserve Board and other bank regulators consider 100% leverage too much of a risk for banks to absorb; and the banking industry sops up all of the treasury's excess debt, as mandated by law!

To get a proper handle on the business of banking, it is important to look at two concepts: leverage and risk.

Leverage

Theoretically, we could set up a bank and promise our customers a savings rate of, say, 3% that will be paid in one year. Let's assume that we are successful in accumulating $1 million of depositor's money. Our bank is now $1 million in debt and in one year will have to pay back depositors a total of $1,030,000 (3%). We then take $100,000 of our depositor's money and purchase United States Treasury Bonds, held by our affiliated Federal Reserve Bank. The next step will be to find good-quality borrowers who are willing to borrow money for one year from our bank at 5%. Remember that we can only loan out 90% of our depositor's money, so our bank kicks in $100,000 from its own equity. We then find qualified customers who will borrow from our bank the full $1 million. At the end of the year, they will have paid us back the original $1 million plus $50,000 (5%) in interest, or $1,050,000. Let's further assume that we cash in our treasury bond and receive $102,000 (2%). So far, our bank has paid back depositors $1,030,000 and has received from borrowers $1,050,000, plus interest from the treasury bond of $2,000.

Now we can calculate how our bank performed. At the end of the year we took in $1,050,000 plus $102,000, totaling $1,152,000. We then paid pack our depositors $1,030,000. And finally, put back into the vaults our equity of $100,000; leaving our bank with a profit of $22,000. If you assume that the bank's Return on Investment (ROI) was 2% of $1,000,000, you would be way off, because the bank's real investment was only $100,000 taken from its equity. Therefore, the actual rate of return was a whopping 22%! This is because the bank was able to leverage its actual investment 10 times -- thanks to our depositor's money.

Risk

Now let's change the scenario and assume that our bank was successful in loaning all $1,000,000, however, we made some shaky loans and $100,000 (10%) of the bank's original portfolio never got paid back. Therefore, instead of receiving $1,050,000 at the end of the year, our bank only received $945,000, which is $900,000, plus interest of $45,000. However, we still had promised to pay our depositors back the full $1,030,000, even though we only received a total of $945,000. This means that we have to dip into our $102,000 of equity, which is still on reserve.

At the end of the year, we took in $945,000, plus $102,000, totaling $1,047,000; then we paid back our depositors $1,030,000 and finally, we put back into the vaults what is left of our $100,000 equity, leaving our bank with a loss of $83,000. Yes, we lost 83% of our equity! Therefore, leverage is a double-edged sword that can earn huge profits, but can also inflict great losses.

Assuming that banks earn a positive return on their loan or investment portfolios, they can use their leverage to dramatically increase profitability. On the other hand, as was discovered in 2008, if they suffer a negative return, through either bad loans or bad investments, they can lose money just as dramatically. And, in 2008 leverage wasn't just ten-to-one, it was twenty and even over thirty-to-one! After banking deregulation, there were still capital requirements to which all of the investment banks needed to adhere; however, in 2004, under pressure from the "Big Banks", the *Net Capital Rule* allowed the brokerage divisions of banks with assets over $5 billion the flexibility of unlimited leverage on investments. And of course, their investments of choice were mortgage-backed securities.

Even in 2013, the largest bank in the United States, JP Morgan Chase Bank, had total assets of $2.42 trillion while its total liabilities were $2.2 trillion, leaving a positive net worth (or equity) of $211 billion. Therefore, its debt-to-worth ratio was 10.4 to 1, or looked at another way, the bank has leveraged its equity, with debt, over 10 times!

To give you a base of comparison: traditionally, if you were a bank credit analyst and you were reviewing the financial statements for one of your business customers, you would like to see a 1 to 1 debt-to-worth ratio, even though several large companies carry higher ratios, 10 to 1 would be considered ridiculously leveraged. In other words, to qualify for a bank loan, the loan officer wants your company's leverage to be one times your equity. A banker may justify this apparent hypocrisy by explaining that bank assets are very secure -- and protected by the federal government. Chase can say to its depositors: "don't worry, your money is safe with us," and it is true, up to $250,000, thanks to the taxpayer-backed FDIC (and, if needed, the likelihood of a Washington bailout); and the borrowers don't care how safe the bank is once they have some of its money. It is the taxpayers of America that care about the safety of our banking system, because if it fails, then the economy crumbles and down comes the entire international house of cards.

It has always been difficult for banks to successfully solicit enough high-quality loans to maximize the leverage on their deposits, which are liabilities on their balance sheet. They therefore successfully lobbied to repeal the *Glass-Steagall Act*, which separated commercial banking activities from investment banking, and the direct investment in securities. This gave banks a new avenue to create and invest in securities like stocks, bonds and a plethora of new exotic investment packages. During the Glass-Steagall era, banks could package and sell their loan portfolios to other banks, called "Loan Participations." However, even that had its risks, as evidenced by the Penn Square Bank fiasco where the bank sold huge participations in bad real estate loans to other unsuspecting banks.

You can see that banks are a heavily leveraged business, and since our tax dollars are paying to insure their deposits it is in our best interests that government regulations assure a safe and financially sound banking system.

Housing Slump

When the 2008 recession hit, the foreclosure rate increased dramatically; the mortgage-backed securities went bust; banks that were heavily invested in these funds lost trillions; new residential construction ground to a halt; more and more bank-held mortgages went into foreclosure; and the Feds stepped in to bail out the banks.

While the banking industry and the Federal Reserve Board are mostly at fault, a large share of the blame belongs to the President, Congress and departments within the federal government. First, had the *Glass-Steagall Act* not been repealed, the Great Recession would likely have been just an ordinary recession, and the banking industry would have recovered much more easily. Second, the Federal Deposit Insurance Corporation (FDIC), the Securities and Exchange Commission (SEC), the Comptroller of Currency, the Federal Reserve Board, and other federal agencies were charged with the regulation and oversight of the banking industry -- in my opinion they were sleeping on the job (or hoping for jobs in the private sector). Third, as mentioned before, de-regulation allowed the industry to veer far away from traditional banking services and into highly speculative investments that unwisely risked the taxpayer's money. Fourth, blame can be placed on federal programs like the Department of Housing and Urban Development (HUD), the Federal Housing Administration (FHA), the Veteran's Administration, (VA) Government National Mortgage Association (Ginnie Mae), Farmer's Home Administration, and similar agencies that are in business to either make or guarantee mortgage loans to individuals who would not qualify according to accepted credit standards. Remember that these programs were operating simultaneously with the unscrupulous lenders.

The result of these programs is that borrowers with negligible down payments and low credit scores entered the housing market.

At What Cost?

- Because these borrowers carried a higher risk, there was a greater probability that foreclosures would result than if the programs did not exist.
- The money loaned to these individuals represented real capital, which is a scarce commodity. In other words, money was taken out of the capital flow that could have been used in a more economically beneficial manner. Therefore, a disproportionate percentage of our nation's wealth went to housing and the banking industry as opposed to other industries. This contributed to the resulting housing bubble. It also caused the building industry to over-expand.

- Quality housing is also a scarce commodity. Less qualified borrowers were competing with more highly qualified borrowers for the same house (higher down payments, better credit scores). This resulted in bidding wars that artificially exaggerated the bubble.
- Because these programs were so popular, there was an increased number of questionable mortgages that would ultimately be foreclosed.
- When the recession hit, along with high rates of unemployment, many marginal borrowers, who under normal conditions could have afforded their mortgage payments, were now being foreclosed.
- Housing prices have to make sense based on the true value of the home. Prices can only go so high before they become unsustainable. Leading up to the housing slump there was a glut of buyers who bid up home prices. However, as prices rose, there were fewer and fewer buyers until eventually -- no buyers.
- Those homeowners who purchased during the bubble and subsequently experienced financial problems, like the loss of a job, reduction in hours, losses in the stock market, unexpected medical expenses, etcetera, could no longer afford their mortgage payments.
- Hundreds of thousands of homeowners found it in their financial best interests to simply walk away from homes that were worth significantly less than their mortgage balance.
- Remember that we are the taxpayers! The federal insurance that protected depositors, was our money. The money that paid for the banking bailout was our money. The mortgages that were made or guaranteed by a federal agency, again our money.
- Federal National Mortgage Association (Fannie Mae) and Federal Home Loan Mortgage (Freddie Mac), both quasi-federal entities, underwrote the majority of mortgages made in America. This enormous federal involvement in the

housing market helped create an artificially high demand, adding to the bubble; and when the housing market crashed, it was taxpayer money that bailed them out.

- The Home Mortgage Interest Deduction. Homeowners with a mortgage were (and are) able to reduce their taxable income by the amount paid in mortgage interest on their principal residences. Therefore, the bigger the house, the more mortgage interest paid; resulting in a bigger tax deduction, which helps subsidize the purchase of bigger and bigger homes. (One result is that middle and upper middle-class homeowners benefit far more than lower income homeowners. Renters, of course, don't receive any of this real estate windfall. I have never heard one economist suggest that this is good public policy. Nor have I ever heard a politician even attempt to justify the obvious unfairness. After all, why should the federal government reward me for taking out a mortgage? Why should the federal government even care if I am renting or buying a home? The answer is that special interests have once again successfully lobbied Congress and the President for favored legislation. Who wins if the federal government subsidizes home purchases? The National Association of Realtors, the American Bankers Association, the National Association of Homebuilders, the Mortgage Bankers Association, American Land Title Association, and others. These are powerful lobbies that spend hundreds of millions of dollars a year to make sure legislation artificially props up home purchases and correspondingly, prices.)
- The *Community Reinvestment Act.* To understand this legislation, we first need to discuss the practice of redlining. It used to be the practice of banks to take a red pen and outline geographical areas where the real estate was unlikely to hold its collateral value. As you might expect, these were typically poor inner-city neighborhoods. The practice of redlining followed the enactment of the *National Housing Act of 1934.*

In 1935, the Federal Home Loan Bank Board (FHLBB) asked Home Owners' Loan Corporation (HOLC) to look at 239 cities and create 'residential security maps' to indicate the level of security for real-estate investments in each surveyed city [1].

Now fast forward to 1977 when it was determined that the practice discriminated against minorities. It wasn't enough to simply ban the practice and monitor compliance. Congress determined that the banking industry needed to make amends (for this government-initiated practice). While the *Community Reinvestment Act* didn't mandate that banks do anything, it was a pressure tactic that threatened to limit a bank's ability to expand unless the bank accrued enough credits for its efforts to engage minority neighborhoods. There were credits for counseling programs, the introduction of bank branches and other direct investments in minority dominated neighborhoods -- but primarily loans, mortgage loans in particular were needed to comply with the new legislation. Even though the act stipulated that only sound credit criteria be used to evaluate applicants, in reality, credit and collateral standards were loosened in an effort to get regulators off the banker's backs. These inner-city loans, at least in the Detroit market, were the first to go bad and when the real estate market turned sour in 2008. City of Detroit real estate values were dropping at over 50% per year, far more pronounced than any of the suburban markets.

- In 2010, the FHA created the *Hardest Hit* program in a handful of states. This program was created to make second and third mortgages, on the same residence, to borrowers in the process of losing their homes to bank foreclosures. The U.S. taxpayer was (and still is) backing these mortgages -- saddling borrowers with additional debt -- in spite of the fact that they couldn't (and can't) afford their existing loans.

Again, looking at Detroit, thousands of these homes were ultimately lost to either first mortgage bank foreclosures or municipal tax foreclosures basically just throwing away taxpayer's money.

What Can Be Done?

Here are a few suggestions. First, the banking industry should return to Glass-Steagall era regulations. Commercial banks should divest their interests in investment banking entities. These spin-offs could become independent entities or be acquired and consolidated by larger investment banks; but they would not be insured or guaranteed by taxpayers. Investment banking and commercial banking are two entirely different business animals, each with its own risks and rewards. There are overlaps, but also potential conflicts of interests, the most important being the desire to maximize profits and, in doing so, the potential of taking excessively high risks. These risks are not only born by the stockholders, but also the taxpayers through the FDIC and Congress in the case of a future bailout. I don't see a problem with banks owning the retail side of investment banking (the stock brokerage business), as well as financial planning services for their wealthy clients. In this capacity, commercial banks would function as independent agents for the investment banking industry.

I would also advise a ten-year phase-out of all government involvement in the mortgage financing business. There is a legitimate function for "Freddie" and "Fannie" type entities, perhaps with some modifications. They could continue to hold large quantities of packaged mortgages and also act as conduits between retail mortgage banking and a resurgence of the private secondary market, which is where mortgages are bundled into mortgage-backed bonds and then sold to investors; this time with only a modest use of derivatives. Under this plan, federal regulators would demand that the mortgages originated by federally insured banks all conform to standard credit and collateral requirements. It would be critically important that investors know the levels of risk associated with these bonds, because if an investment goes bust, taxpayers will once again be on the hook. Private lenders, on the other hand would be free to risk their own capital on less qualified mortgage borrowers, and even bundle these mortgages into high risk bonds that could be sold to investors who would be fully aware of the risk.

Today, over 60% of all mortgages are backed by the government in some way, primarily by Freddie Mac, Fannie Mae, HUD, VA, or USDA Rural Development Mortgages. The mortgage defaults which began in 2008 completely wiped out the solvency of both Freddie Mac and Fannie Mae. This caused the Federal Government to inject $170 billion into these entities, which was the costliest government bailout in history. At the present time, taxpayers have been paid back; however, it appears that Fannie and Freddie' stockholders will never see a dime of their investment, instead, all profits ($20 billion in 2016) are sent to the Treasury Department's General Fund. This means that, at least for now, the two entities are nothing more than highly profitable, de facto government agencies.

CHAPTER SEVEN

Taxism: The Problem with High Taxes

Tis impossible to be sure of anything but Death and Taxes
The Cobbler of Preston by Christopher Bullock

In the U.S. and most other modern economies, the private sector primarily controls the means of production as profit-seeking, capitalist entities. Private capital is raised for new business ventures and if properly managed, the marketplace determines their success or failure. If unsuccessful, then the investors and lenders will lose their invested or loaned funds. If on the other hand the businesses are successful, then the loans will be re-paid and the profits will be used to enrich the entrepreneurs and/or be re-invested to grow their businesses. As profits grow, taxes are paid and employees are hired. Capital investment also grows as new buildings, equipment and inventory are purchased. Suppliers and their employees benefit as do all who fractionally benefit from the economic expansion. The prosperity that results from this process enhances a society's ability to support needed government programs and charitable endeavors.

Does it matter if money originates from the private sector or the public sector? Money circulates through the economy exactly the same regardless of where it comes from; however, money that originates from the public sector is dependent on tax revenues. Therefore, as taxpayers, we should expect that our national quality of life and/or security interests are enhanced by that dollar and that every public-sector employee accepts a fiduciary responsibility to utilize that dollar in the most effective and efficient manner possible. Going back to my original premise: it doesn't really matter if products or services are provided by public or private entities. What matters is if they provide more in value to customers, taxpayers, and society than their costs.

Tax Rates

The United States has the third highest general top marginal corporate income tax rate in the world, at 38.92 percent (consisting of the 35% federal rate plus a combined state rate). Due to the recent reduction in Chad's corporate tax rate, the U.S. rate is exceeded only by the United Arab Emirates and Puerto Rico (a U.S. Territory). The worldwide average top corporate income tax rate, across 188 countries and tax jurisdictions, is 22.5 percent.

Taxfoundation.org

Congress determined, that among other considerations, the U.S. was at a tax disadvantage when trading internationally and has therefore, lowered the top corporate tax rate to 20%. High tax rates may result in a short-term boost to revenues, but long term they decrease economic activity which will consequently decrease tax revenues and increase the social costs of unemployment. Conversely, low stable tax rates increase beneficial economic activity, which results in long term economic growth and ultimately, higher tax revenues.

Congress finally figured out that the public sector relies on a healthy private sector to provide tax revenues, which in turn pay for government services. If my taxes are increased, then by the same margin my income or purchasing power is decreased. Therefore, as tax rates increase there is less incentive for entrepreneurs to grow their businesses, or employees to work harder to advance their careers, or for multinational corporations to invest at home, if the government is simply going to take a higher percentage of their growing incomes. Also, tax rates that are higher than our trading partners will contribute to a tendency by multinational corporations to avoid high domestic tax rates by investing in production facilities abroad. High tax rates discourage domestic investment and encourage investment in low-tax nations. The profits from those investments are often kept and re-invested offshore.

Tax Inversions

> *Companies who enjoy the benefits of doing business in America should help pay for the costs of America by paying U.S. taxes. It's wrong to be able to change your address to avoid paying U.S. taxes...*
> Former Treasury Secretary, Jack Lew (1955-),
> CNBC Closing Bell, April 14, 2016

Congress also eliminated the need by U.S. Corporations to reincorporate a company overseas to reduce the tax burden on income earned abroad. These are the effects:

- In certain sectors, companies were competing globally against competitors who were paying significantly less in taxes. Therefore, big U.S. multinational companies needed some form of tax equalization to compete on a level playing field.
- Most countries tax their companies once -- when that money is repatriated. A multinational U.S. based company pays the tax twice. Once in the country where the transaction took place and again in the United States when the money is repatriated. (It should be noted that The U.S. has reciprocal tax treaties with some countries intended to avoid the double taxation issue.)
- Unlike tax law in most developed nations, the U.S. Internal Revenue Code imposes income tax on the profits of American corporations' foreign subsidiaries. This created

a strong incentive for American companies with large overseas markets to recharacterize themselves as foreign corporations.

> *The incentive is simple. America taxes profits no matter where they are earned, at a rate of 39% (including the average state tax) — higher than in any other rich country. When a company becomes foreign through a merger, or 'inverts', it no longer owes American tax on its foreign profit. It still owes American tax on its American profit."*
> "Inverse logic", The Economist,
> Washington, D.C., 20 September 2014

- Even though shareholders and managers would prefer that their money be invested back home and in American dollars, U.S. tax policy encouraged multinationals to keep their foreign earnings invested offshore where it could accumulate faster.

Even though Congress is moving in the right direction, more can be done. In addition to lowering corporate taxes, we could make certain reinvested earnings tax-exempt. This would not include foreign investments or the acquisition of existing companies, but would be focused on investments in domestic plants, equipment, inventory, and employees. There could also be a tax credit for multinational companies that move investments from foreign countries to the United States. Creating incentives to invest at home would definitely help to grow Gross Domestic Product (GDP) while simultaneously reducing unemployment.

Dividend Income

Tax rates on wages are relatively higher than on dividends. But corporate dividends are paid on after tax dollars, and are therefore taxed twice. First, corporate profits are taxed at the companies normal tax rate; and second, if the corporation decides to distribute a portion of its profits back to the owners, then those dividends are taxed again. For this reason, many smaller companies don't incorporate; instead they form Limited Liability Companies that function exactly like corporations, except that there is no corporate tax liability.

There is a misconception that low dividend tax rates only benefit the rich and should therefore be raised. In reality, most dividends are paid through mutual funds to older Americans to supplement Social Security and other retirement income.

Capital Gains

Many people believe that the capital gains tax should be increased; but before you agree, perhaps it would be a good idea to look at the facts through the following example. First, someone purchases an asset with after tax dollars; then, if that asset increases in value, and he sells the asset at its new higher price, he is taxed again on its gain; and he is taxed at his normal rate, unless he holds the asset for over a year at which time he is taxed typically at 15%, which is probably lower than his normal tax rate. While there is no limit to the upside of his *taxable* long-term capital gains income, there is a serious limit to the amount of income that he can shelter from his losses. Losses can offset capital gains or other income, however only to a maximum annual limit of $1,500 for an individual or $3,000 for a married couple. Therefore, if an individual loses $30,000 in one year, it will take 20 years to finally write off all of the losses! Not such a great deal when you consider that in 2015 nearly 70% of investors lost money in the stock market.

How Do Taxes Benefit Me?

As a taxpayer, I want my overall taxes to be as low as possible, relative to the vast array of government services for which I have paid. For example, when I turn on the tap, I expect drinkable water to start flowing. When I drive to work, I expect the roads to be in good repair. If my house catches fire, I expect the fire department to promptly arrive and put it out. Therefore, with state and local taxes there is a noticeable correlation between what I pay and what I see the government doing. I know that my gas tax is going to road repair, my property tax to education and other local services, my water and sewer bill to -- water and sewer. With the federal government, however, there is a far less direct relationship between me and the services that it provides. Federal money is thrown all over the world and in so many different programs that it boggles the imagination. And unfortunately, too much of the money is funneled to special-interest groups as directed by one of 13,000 registered Washington DC lobbyists. Yes, federal lobbying is a $3.5 billion industry, and the career path for too many congressmen, senators, and government officials. No wonder the average working American looks at the size and scope of the federal government and asks: "I pay taxes, but what does the federal government do for me?"

CHAPTER EIGHT

Protectionism: Who Wins and Who Loses?

*When a country (USA) is losing many billions of dollars
on trade with virtually every country it does business
with, trade wars are good, and easy to win.*
Donald Trump, March 2, 2018 (Twitter)

There is a common misperception that exports are good for a nation and imports bad. It is better, however, to think of imports and exports as two sides of the same coin. Every mutually beneficial transaction, whether domestic or international, increases the well-being of both the buyer and the seller -- regardless of whether an American is the buyer or the seller. Now, if you multiply this concept by all the transactions in the world, then you have increased both the wealth and well-being of the entire planet.

International Trade

The United States contains fewer than 5% of the world's population, yet we consume about 27% of the world's GDP. It's not surprising then that in this country we consume more than we produce. Therefore, we import more goods than we export, causing what is called a "Trade Deficit." Politicians complain vigorously about this deficit, believing that it means some other country is stealing our jobs and enriching itself at our expense (reminiscent of Mercantilist

Protectionism). Let's see if this is true by taking a look at the topic of international finance.

There are two components to international trade. The first is the relationship between the value of my country's currency to the value of my trading partner's currency. The second component is the value of the product, commodity or service to be sold. If I live in a country with a strong currency, I prefer to purchase products from a country with a weak currency because my strong currency is relatively more valuable. This makes the cost of products from that country cheaper. On the other hand, if I want to export products from my strong currency country to a weak currency country, then my products will be more expensive because my customer in the weak currency country has to spend more of his less valuable currency to compensate me for my more expensive currency. Therefore, strong currencies encourage imports and weak currencies encourage exports.

The reason for currency variations is "Fiat Money." Unlike in the past when all nation's currencies were backed by a commodity like gold or silver with an established commonly accepted value, currencies today are backed by the full faith and credit of the issuing nations. The Foreign Exchange Market (Forex), which is the largest marketplace in the world, oversees continually fluctuating prices, or "Exchange Rates," for all trading partners in the exchange. The exchange rate is an exact denominational relationship between two currencies. Strong currencies are typically backed by fiscally strong governments with tight monetary policies; weak currencies are backed by fiscally weaker governments, or with looser monetary policies. Therefore, even the strongest, most fiscally sound governments are able to manipulate the value of their currencies by raising or lowering interest rates. High interest rates reduce the amount of currency in circulation by increasing the cost of money, low interest rates have the opposite effect, flooding the financial markets with cheap money. Therefore, if a government's policy is to make imported products cheap, thereby increasing it's consumer's wealth, then policymakers will raise interest rates and maintain tight monetary policy. On the other hand, if policymakers wish to encourage exports, thereby protecting domestic producers and workers, then they maintain loose monetary policies. They also might include high tariff rates, import restrictions, domestic content requirements and subsidies for domestic producers. Keep in mind, however, that the main reason countries trade with each other is because it is mutually beneficial for both parties.

The U.S. imports oil from Canada, Saudi Arabia and other countries primarily because the price of oil on world markets (including the U.S.) is normally cheaper than the costs related to domestic exploration, leasing or purchasing oil rich properties and drilling new wells to meet 100% of the U.S. oil demand. We also have a huge appetite for consumer goods. Therefore, to the extent that we can purchase them cheaper from say, Chinese, Southeast Asian or Mexican manufacturers than from domestic manufacturers, our standard of living improves in exact proportion to the money that we have saved by purchasing their comparable, but cheaper products.

Let's say hypothetically that my computer dies, so I go to an electronics store and look at two computers of similar quality, one built in China and one built in the U.S.; but the Chinese computer costs $100.00 less. If I purchase the Chinese computer, then I have $100.00 more in my pocket than if I purchased the American product, which means that by purchasing the cheaper computer, I am $100.00 richer. If you multiply this by similar examples, then millions of consumers are purchasing a variety of imported products, saving in aggregate trillions of dollars! Therefore, it is pretty easy to see the positive effect imported products have on our general standard of living. This is not to disparage our domestic producers, because there are many examples where our companies can out-compete foreign competitors. But, too often an uncompetitive U.S. manufacturer, demanding protection, will complain to Congress that his company can't compete, for example, with China because of unfair business practices, lax government regulations, child labor, currency manipulation -- or China subsidizes a government controlled business's losses, which allow them to subsequently "dump" their products at artificially low prices in order to put our company out of business – leading them to dramatically increase prices and control the market.

Do these arguments against the Chinese (or any other country) hold any water? First, child labor: It wasn't until 1938 that the *Fair Labor Standards Act* was passed by Congress. This was the first federal law regulating child labor that was upheld by the Supreme Court. And even then, certain industries, such as agriculture and newspaper publishing were excluded. In 2006, the National Agriculture Statistics Service released a report indicating that 431,730 youths, aged 12- to 17-years-old, were hired for agricultural work. Even more troubling is that according to the National Safety Council, due to pesticides and a high rate of injury, agriculture is considered the second most dangerous occupation in the United States. Finally, under U.S. law, children on farms can work at age 12 for unlimited hours before and after school.

How about currency manipulation? After the Great Recession, the Federal Reserve Board initiated Quantitative Easing (QE): this policy involved the massive purchases of long-term Government Securities. The goal was to keep interest rates low to stimulate the economy. The secondary effect of the Fed's purchase of trillions of dollars of debt was that the value of the U.S. dollar went down relative to other foreign currencies, which through government intervention made American exports artificially cheap. This, in effect, was currency manipulation by the United States Government. Other Organization for Economic Co-operation and Development (OECD) nations followed, resulting in a currency war; similar in effect to a trade war. These countries also wanted to increase exports and bolster their economies, so they all executed their own versions of QE. And while currency manipulation by the U.S. ended in 2014, so did China. According to an April 11, 2017 *New York Times* article "Since the middle of 2014 it (China) has sold over $1 trillion from its reserves to prop up the Renminbi, under pressure from capital flight by Chinese companies and savers." If we really want to blame China for currency manipulation, then we need to look at the period from 2005 to 2009. It was during this pre-Great Recession period that China appeared to purposefully devalue its currency in order to artificially inflate exports. Yet as recent as April 2, 2017, President Trump told the *Financial Times:* "When you talk about currency manipulation, when you talk about devaluations, (the Chinese) are world champions." A legitimate criticism of the Chinese relates to their almost complete disregard for intellectual property rights.

Finally, what about the government ownership of major exporters? After 2008, the United States government bailed-out General Motors and Chrysler, effectively taking ownership control of both companies. By the summer of 2009, the federal government of the United States owned a 60% stake in the new General Motors after the company emerged from Chapter 11 bankruptcy. President Obama even fired GM's chairman, Rick Wagoner. In a March 30, 2009 article, *Wired.com* writes:

> *The bottom line is Uncle Sam told Wagoner he'd have to take a hike if the floundering automaker was to get any more cash out of taxpayers. In addition to telling Wagoner to hit the bricks, the Obama administration wants to push Chrysler into a shotgun wedding with Fiat — or any other suitor that comes along.*

As a matter of fact, there was eventually a deal between Chrysler and Fiat. Our federal government gave the UAW a 17% stake in GM and a 55% share of Chrysler. Politics matter! The UAW thanked Obama in the 2012 election by giving him decisive victories in key electoral districts of Ohio and Michigan. The auto bailouts ultimately cost the United States taxpayers approximately $9.3 billion. While the U.S. government is now out of the auto business, it is not inconceivable (or unconstitutional) that a future President may take complete control of a major U.S. manufacturer.

Tariffs

Going back to my hypothetical computer example: if Congress were to mandate a $100.00 tariff on every Chinese made computer sold in America, then each one of countless consumers would be $100.00 poorer. On the other hand, the American manufacturer does not need to become more productive and still is millions of dollars richer, because Congress has mandated that United States computer consumers must subsidize his company. Congress wins too, because for every one of our hypothetical Chinese computer sold in America, they collect an invisible tax of $100.00. Further, let's assume that this action angers China so they retaliate by placing bigger tariffs on totally different American exports to China, hurting other U.S. exporters, and thus the trade war has begun. The results, which are universally bad, wind up hurting both economies. I should also mention that the only entities able to successfully lobby Congress for tariff protection are politically-connected companies and big unions, in other words, those who invest millions of dollars in political campaign donations. If, from a public policy standpoint, tariffs are such a good idea, then why not set a standard tariff rate applicable to all products equally? The answer of course is that an international trade war would ensue, resulting in a second Great Depression. And if, as a nation, we are serious about child labor abuses, then why should U.S. law exempt agriculture and newspaper publishing? The answer, of course, is that big agribusiness and news organizations are too politically powerful. Therefore, in the case of agriculture, they get to enjoy exemptions from child labor laws, gifts in the form of government subsidies, and trade protections such as tariffs and other import restrictions.

As previously mentioned, a communist country is able to control commerce within its own borders, however, it has no control over the international marketplace. The same concept is true in the United States. Our government can and does control the price we pay for all imported products. These protectionist practices provide benefits to those industries with political clout, but only in regard to the domestic market, which is about 20% of the global marketplace. Therefore, if you are only competitive at home because of government protections and/ or subsidies, then your company is missing out on 80% of its potential market. Once the company attempts to export its products to another country, suddenly it has no U.S. government protection and must be competitive globally. Otherwise it will fail as an exporter. And if it does fail, what happens to the workers back home that would have been hired, or the factories, raw materials and equipment that would have been built or purchased? All this potential economic activity can never be realized because the company wasn't forced by the marketplace to continually improve quality and customer service; while at the same time reducing costs through better efficiency and production methods. And as previously mentioned, when other countries impose retaliatory import restrictions against U.S. products, we are even less competitive. As a logical consequence, many U.S. companies don't export, they simply manufacture in countries other than the U.S. for the world's markets (where they must be internationally competitive) and their U.S. plants only serve U.S. customers, greatly limiting the manufacturing job opportunities at home.

I realize that there are several countries around the globe that impose stringent import restrictions against the United States, which therefore breeds retaliation. I also realize that the United States has joined with other countries, and regional blocks of countries in free trade agreements. However, the result is a series of piecemeal trade agreements, treaties, and punitive policies that wind up benefiting some countries and industries at the expense of others, and make some products artificially cheap, some artificially expensive and some completely unavailable. In other words, the international marketplace is a hodgepodge of mostly bad policies that generally hurt U.S. consumers and producers, as well as our trading partners. Again, it comes back to government policies that are created based on political considerations rather than policies that encourage maximizing value for the American consumer and the American taxpayer.

If another country wants to export products to the United States and they happen to be outside of a free trade zone, these are some of the tariff rates that they will have to pay at the border: sugar 26%, cars and tractors 12.5% to 25%, televisions 29%, shavers 35%, bicycles 35% to 41%, baby carriages 49%, and running shoes 35%.

A reasonable person may ask: why not bring all the major players of the world together and establish a unified free trade policy that is fair to all, including punishments for the cheaters? Why not create an international umbrella organization that would monitor and administer the policy? And, why couldn't the United States take a lead role in spearheading this great idea? The answer can be summed up with two concepts: Politics and American Exceptionalism! Politicians need the money from donations, which come from individuals and organizations that benefit from the current system. And, America resists being part of any international organization that places it in a subordinate position. Our politicians want complete freedom of action without answering to anyone, even if the action is stupid, self-serving, counter-productive, violates international law, or lacks any semblance of common sense. Perhaps it is time for us to put in place a stronger constitution that forces politicians to help develop and abide by international rules and norms that would apply to every nation -- including the United States.

Fiat Money and International Debt

Under the old European system of international finance, trade deficits were paid in actual shipments of gold or silver. If your country didn't have enough gold in its treasury to cover the deficit, then you could try to borrow enough gold from an international "Merchant Banker" to cover your deficit. If you were unsuccessful, then no other country would accept your currency.

Under the current system, trade deficits are different than fiscal deficits in that trade deficits are not debt, they never have to be repaid. Hypothetically, however, if the United States had no exports, then there would be no dollars in international circulation. Therefore, if a U.S. company wanted to import products from abroad, then the U.S. importer would have to trade something of equivalent value or; if the foreign exporter were willing, accept dollars in payment, then come to the United States and purchase something of equivalent value.

Propping-up the Dollar

U.S. politicians concerned with American jobs love exports and hate imports but become particularly vocal against countries with whom we carry a balance of trade deficit. In the cases of China and the EU, in 2016 alone, we carried combined balance of trade deficits of $494 billion. If both countries suddenly stopped buying U.S. assets and sold all their U.S. dollars on the international currencies exchange, the market would suddenly be flooded with dollars, which would dramatically lower the dollar's FOREX exchange rate value, relative to the Renminbi and Euro, making their exports to the U.S. far costlier for American consumers. This is obviously not a good thing for countries that want to export lots of stuff to us. Therefore, it is in the best interests of all our trading partners to keep the dollar strong; in fact, the stronger our economy the better for them. If in the process, they artificially prop up the value of the U.S. dollar, then it is okay with them. In our case, U.S. banks and U.S. treasury notes are still considered among the safest in the world -- which is a terrible indictment of the ability of the world's governments to manage their finances.

Foreign Trade Statistics

In 2012, we imported about $2.74 trillion worth of goods and services and exported about $2.2 trillion, creating a trade deficit of about $540 billion. In that same year, $5.5 trillion or 34% of our $16 trillion federal debt was held by foreign nations.

Now, let's take a minute to examine this enormous foreign debt and can ask two questions: First, if we had no federal debt, would the $5.5 trillion instead be invested in U.S. assets, which would translate into an increase in American jobs? The answer is yes, at least a good chunk of it. And second, why do these countries loan us so much money? To answer the second question -- consider the countries in which we carry a balance of trade deficit as creditor nations when they purchase U.S. Treasury bonds. Then let's compare these creditor nations to a manufacturer whose best customer, in our hypothetical example, is developing financial problems. The manufacturer wants to keep selling him products, but is starting to get a little nervous about his ability to pay down his line of credit, which continues to grow beyond any reasonable expectation of repayment. You could force him into bankruptcy and get perhaps pennies on the dollar for your debt -- but, the customer continues to pay you interest and keeps buying your products, so in spite of your better judgment you decide to carry his debt indefinitely.

It is important to note that we have the world's most powerful military, which gives us a lot of clout in international finance. No foreign power is able to come along and bully the United States into accepting a disadvantageous trade agreement. We, on the other hand can force international or unilateral sanctions against any disagreeable nation we choose. Our powerful military is in the background to act as a club if necessary. In fact, currently we have trade sanctions against a total of seventeen countries, and trade is absolutely prohibited with Belarus, Cuba, Eritrea, Iran, North Korea, Syria, and Venezuela; unless of course, our government decides to make specific exceptions.

Currency Confusion

There currently are 164 different national currencies and each one of these nations would prefer to receive payment for their exports in their local currency. China would rather have all payments made in the Renminbi and the EU countries would like to be paid with Euro. In fact, international finance would be greatly simplified if there were only one currency in use by all countries; however, who would be willing to back such a currency? A singular worldwide currency would require a one-world governing body to back it; and of course, the coordination of 197 independent nations would be a political and fiscal nightmare! The other option is to revert to a system where all currencies would be backed by commodities like gold or silver, but as we have seen throughout history, a system of commodity-backed currencies is less than perfect.

Interdependent or Codependent

In international finance, there is the additional complication of economic interdependence. Any given country may have millions of jobs dependent on exports to the United States. Let's assume hypothetically that you are the Prime Minister of Canada and your country's corporations have millions of parts manufactured in America. They may have, in aggregate, trillions of dollars of investments in this country and trillions of dollars invested by U.S. companies in Canada. Your Canadian banks may have invested trillions in U.S. bonds, securities, inter-bank participations, branches, and accounts. The bottom line is that if the United States goes down, Canada goes down and so does the rest of the world! The problem isn't our balance of trade deficit, it's the soundness of our currency that is used as an unsecured loan in international transactions; which relates directly to the strength of the issuing entity -- the U.S. federal government.

The Third World

I would like to start this topic with the following premise: there is no reason that the whole world cannot be as prosperous as the United States, and, there is no limit to the potential economic growth of the United States. The human population of our planet (currently at about 7.5 billion) is miniscule compared to its capacity, not only to sustain life, but to allow for every human on this earth to live a life in comfort and good health. But unfortunately, in many parts of the world we have squandered our natural resources and governments have used political and military force to subjugate the many while enriching the few.

The Modern Third World

In the 1970's and 1980's more than 90% of economic aid to the third world went to massive power plants; however, in many cases there was no fuel to run the power plants and except for roads, there was no infrastructure, no skilled labor or qualified management, no replacement equipment or spare parts if something broke down, and even if there had been, there was no maintenance personnel to fix the problems. Aid agencies were also clueless as to the international market niches that could be supplied by the products of third world countries. How then, could these economic weaklings develop into western-style industrial behemoths?

The simple answer is that we didn't want the industrial competition or cheap labor that was and is abundant in the third world. What we wanted was compliant non-communist countries that wouldn't nationalize their natural resources and would vote as desired by the U.S. when it came to the United Nations. Therefore, while our political leaders preached the ideals of democracy, our espionage agencies were instructed to topple democratically elected communist leaders in favor of authoritarian military thugs who could be bought with American dollars. In return, we were assured of cheap raw materials and agricultural products. The result was continued third world poverty, repression and subjugation. We replaced colonialism with an equally brutal neocolonialism that continues to exist today. And, unfortunately, those countries that did turn communist were often ruled by a different set of military thugs. Congo, Ethiopia, Mozambique, North Korea, Venezuela and Cuba are some current examples.

What the West failed to realize, however, was that in Sub-Saharan Africa alone, there is a population of almost one billion people. That means one billion potential new consumers with purchasing power. Just imagine the export opportunities for the United States. Not to mention the increased standard of living and quality of life for the African people.

Why Power Plants?

In some cases, they were needed to more efficiently extract, process and ship natural resources, as in the colonial era. In other cases, they were desired by the country's elites in order to have modern conveniences. But in most cases, they were simply a way to funnel billions of dollars to big United States-based (and politically connected) construction, engineering, and consulting firms. The process worked sort of like this: consulting firms would send teams of economists to third world countries. The purpose was to evaluate the long-term economic benefits to various countries of building hydroelectric plants. The economists would write reports that were intended to sell the idea to the World Bank of loaning billions of dollars to third world dictators, who cared very little about economic development, but cared very deeply about billions of dollars. The reports were very detailed and accurate in describing a country's current situation and the estimated costs of building a proposed power plant -- but when estimating the economic impact of the investment and true benefits to the people, the reports were entirely self-serving and fictitious [2].

By 1994, third world debt was approximately $1.2 trillion, with interest accruing at $50 billion every year. Today, that debt has been cut in half, but is still economically crushing. Instead of raising overall standards of living, the money went to increase the wealth of third world elites, and to build hydroelectric plants that were never intended to power industrial awakenings. Instead of repaying the debt from business expansion, countries were forced to pay creditors by stripping and selling-off their natural resources.

What About International Aid?

Contrary to popular opinion, charity inhibits economic growth. First, if someone is willing to give you something for free, why work? Second, if you ship tons of free clothes, then local textile mills will never need to exist. Third, if you ship tons of free food, local farmers will go out of business. Finally, when the foreign aid ceases or is delayed, those in dependency will starve. Relief agencies are important as stop gap and emergency measures to provide food, medical attention and other necessities, however, much of the third world has become permanently dependent on the 3.7 million Non-Government Organizations (NGO's) that control trillions of dollars from governments and other donors. What third world countries need is to be economically, politically and socially unshackled from the chains of oppression and war.

In the new millennia, reforms have been made, but the centuries of colonialism, neocolonialism, repression and subjugation have left an open wound on the third world that has not healed.

In the book, *Why Nations Fail: The Origins of Power, Prosperity, and Poverty*, Daron Acemoglu and James A. Robinson argue that nations and their inhabitants are poor because for centuries they have been forced to survive under oppressive government regimes. They are not poor due to climate, geography, or innate human characteristics that are different from people in richer nations.

Human Nature

Every human on this planet shares a common ancestor. We are so closely related genetically that if we were dogs, we would all be the same breed. (*Races* are not even recognized as biologically valid entities.) In fact, scientists have now concluded that the DNA inherent in every human on earth is approximately 99.5% identical and that most of the variation is from humans within their respective populations! Therefore, while we are all members of the human race, we are also divided into several distinct racial groups, and within each race are sub-groups. Then of course each individual has inherited from his or her parents their own personalized genetic characteristics. That being said, the differences in culture, religion, language, and values are far more significant than the genetics of race or ethnicity. For example, a baby adopted from Korea by American parents will, as a teenager, behave and sound like every other average American teenager. On the other hand, the same Korean baby if raised in Korea will, as a teenager, behave and sound like every other Korean teenager.

As we mature, our brains are wired to be part of a group, similar to a dog's brain, which is wired to be part of a pack. Therefore, it is a part of human nature to organize into groups, or what I refer to here as **Collectives**. Therefore, we can think of collectives as nothing more than extensions of our tribal instincts that developed over the 200 thousand years of our existence as a species. A side effect of this process is a collectivized form of "Ego-centrism." Meaning that in diverse societies we cling to and trust those who are most similar to ourselves. In other words, those who look like us, sound like us and share the same values, religion and culture. Of course, this doesn't mean that individuals, families, and other groups can't and don't cross racial, religious, or cultural bounds, but it does mean that they must find common threads that bind them together, superseding the differences, whatever they may be.

In spite of the fact that we are all born equal in the eyes of God and nature, our ego/collective-centric tendencies drive illogical feelings of superiority. We feel that our religion, political party, ethnicity, nationality, organizational affiliations, sports teams, sex, sexual orientation, tribes, clans, class, family, values and ideas (I consider all of the above collectives.) are the best, the most-right and the most-valid. And that our needs supersede the needs of others. Our competitive/territorial spirit cause us (at least to attempt) to dominate, convert, defeat, control or in extreme cases destroy competing collectives. Interestingly, we can easily detect these tendencies in others, but are often blind to our own collective/ego-centric inclinations. These factors, plus a quest by some for wealth and power, have caused almost all human struggles and political agendas. It is worthwhile to note that the same tendencies we demonstrate through human nature as individuals are extrapolated to collectives, since they are nothing more than groups of individuals.

The path to world peace and world prosperity is simple. In 1990's parlance, we all just need to "get over ourselves." Those in power need to fight their own collective/ego-centric tendencies and ask the question what is best, not just for me and my collective, but for society and all humanity?

Of course, the United States is incapable of meeting all the welfare needs of the world and we cannot be responsible for remediating every evil. We should also remember that it is our tax dollars that fund the functionings of the United States government. Therefore, providing for the welfare, security and prosperity of U.S. citizens should be the first priority. With that being said, however, there is still an enormous amount of good that we can do around the world.

So, what role should the United States play in defending and enhancing world peace and in the process, international prosperity? The first is redefining our national interests to those that respect all people's rights of self-determination instead of politically-based alliances. The second is strengthening international legal, economic and political bodies. The third is the gradual squeezing out of oppressive governments. The fourth is to support international efforts to peacefully fill political vacuums. The fifth is to encourage *value-based* governments and *value-based* economic systems to create *value-based* societies around the world. Finally, all governments need to respect private property, encourage foreign investment, foster entrepreneurship, invest in both infrastructure and education, levy fair and predictable taxes, provide for equal treatment under the law, vigorously engage in foreign trade, and then leave their people alone.

Glossary

Division of Labor: is essentially the breaking down of large jobs into many tiny components in order to increase efficiency.

The Greater Fool Theory: is the irrational notion that in a rising market the intrinsic value of a stock or commodity doesn't matter so long as a bigger or greater fool is willing to pay the investor a higher price at some point in the future.

Aggregate Demand: is defined as the total of Consumer Spending (plus) Capital Investment (plus) government spending (minus) transfer payments like welfare benefits and government pensions (plus or minus) the net difference between exports and Imports (exports minus imports).

Gross Domestic Product: is a monetary measure of the market value of all final goods and services produced in a period (quarterly or yearly) of time, within the United States.

Inflation: is too much money (including debt generated money) chasing too few goods, resulting in a general increase in the price of goods and services. Therefore, a nation's money supply grows faster than its Gross Domestic Product (GDP), which is the annual monetary value of all goods and services produced in the United States. If, for example, the GDP is growing at 2% and the amount of currency flowing through the economy is growing at 4%, then the 2% difference is potentially inflationary.

Multiplier Effect: is where an initial change in aggregate demand can have a much greater final impact on the level of equilibrium national income. This comes about because injections of demand into the circular flow of income stimulate further rounds of spending – in other words, one person's spending is another person's income – and this can theoretically lead to a much bigger effect on equilibrium output and employment.

Recession: is when the national Gross Domestic Product (GDP) is in a contraction (decline in economic activity) for three consecutive quarters.

Stagflation: is persistent high inflation combined with high unemployment and stagnant demand in a country's economy.

Loan Participation: is an arrangement under which a lender originates a loan or package of loans, and while continuing to service the loans, sells all or a portion of these loans to a participating lender or several lenders who accept the risk for these loans, as well as their share of the interest and income flows from the borrowers, as they pay down the debt.

Collective: For the lack of a better word and for the purpose of this book I am using this term, not only in communist terminology, but in reference to all forms of sociological associations.

Notes

CHAPTER ONE

1 http://en.wikipedia.org/wiki/Jean-Baptiste_Colbert
2 Lawrence Reed, President of FEE, discusses Adam Smith's role in the development of economic thought. Mr. Reed outlines how Smith's background in moral philosophy led to his pioneering the study of economics. This lecture was given during the 2011 FEE Summer Seminars, July 24, 2012.
3 For more information, see lecture series: *The Great Courses, The History of the United States, The Great War for Empire*, Allen C. Guelzo, The Teaching Company, LLC
4 Ibid
5 Ibid
6 Ibid
7 Landes, David S., *The Wealth and Poverty of Nations Why Some Nations are so rich and some so poor*, 1998, W.W. Norton Company, Inc., New York, NY
8 Lawrence Reed, President of FEE, 2011 FEE Summer Seminars, July 24, 2012.
9 Ibid
10 Ibid
11 Ibid

CHAPTER TWO

1 SparkNotes Editors. *SparkNote on The Communist Manifesto*. SparkNotes. com. SparkNotes LLC. n.d... Web. 17 Jan. 2013
2 White, Matthew, *The Great Big Book of Horrible Things*, 2011, W.W. Norton & Company, New York.

CHAPTER THREE

1   For more information, see: Jonah Goldberg, Liberal *Fascism, The Secret History of the American Left, from Mussolini to the Politics of Change* (Broadway Books, an imprint of The Crown Publishing Group, a Division of Random House, Inc. New York, 2007)

2   These statistics were taken from: Milton and Rose D. Friedman, *Free to Choose* (Harcourt Brace Jovanovich, Inc., New York, 1979, 1980)

3   Folsom, Burton Jr., *New Deal or Raw Deal? How FDR's Economic Legacy Has Damaged America* (Threshold Editions, a Division of Simon & Schuster, Inc., New York, 2008). Pages 104 – 107.

4   Ibid, Page 44

5   Ibid, Page 44

6   Ibid, Page 62

7   Ibid, Page 67

8   Ibid, Page 82

9   Ibid, Page 83

10   Ibid, Page 86

11   Ibid, Page 87

12   Ibid, Page 171

13   Ibid, Page 87

14   Folsom, Burton W., Jr., https://www.hillsdale.edu/educational-outreach/free-market-forum/2006-archive/fdr-and-the-irs/

CHAPTER EIGHT

1   Zywicki, Todd, Copyright (c) 2014 National Affairs, Inc., The Auto Bailout and the Rule of Law, Issue 7, Spring 2011.

2   Perkins, John, 2004 *Confessions of an Economic Hit Man*, 2006, Plume, a member of Penguin Group (USA), Inc.

About the Author

 A lifelong political and economics junkie, Daniel Cameron has over four decades of professional, management and consulting experience in banking, manufacturing and real estate.

Mr. Cameron holds a Bachelor's degree in Business Administration from Hillsdale College and a Master's degree in Management from Aquinas College. He has taught as adjunct faculty for Grand Valley State University and Davenport University, and has been a speaker at several seminars and corporate events.

Mr. Cameron lives in metropolitan Phoenix with his wife Jessica and their pet boxer Bettye.

Printed in the United States
By Bookmasters